All good wishes
Muriel Best
Williamsburg November 1997

D·E·S·I·G·N S·O·U·R·C·E·S
F·O·R E·M·B·R·O·I·D·E·R·Y

MURIEL BEST AND VICKY LUGG

B.T. Batsford Ltd, London

ISBN 0 7134 5573 X

Typeset by Tek-Art Ltd Kent
and printed and bound in Great Britain by
Anchor Brendon Ltd
Tiptree, Essex
for the publishers
B.T. Batsford Ltd.
4 Fitzhardinge Street
London W1H 0AH

C·O·N·T·E·N·T·S

A·C·K·N·O·W·L·E·D·G·E·M·E·N·T·S

During the preparation of this book so many people have given generously of their help that it is impossible to mention and thank everyone individually. However, we are indebted to Audrey MacLeod for her contribution to Chapter 4; and to our principal photographer Jim Pascoe, whose patience, skill and good humour have been invaluable in recording the great variety of embroideries so kindly lent by friends and colleagues. We must also thank our families for their interest and support; artists Eileen Hogan and the Boyle Family for allowing us to use illustrations of their work; and lastly our editor, Rachel Wright, who has been most understanding and sympathetic.

I·N·T·R·O·D·U·C·T·I·O·N

Although it can be an interesting discipline to work through one idea, basing one's work on a particular theme, perhaps natural form, it is all too easy to repeat a formula until the idea ceases to develop and the result lacks spontaneity.

The purpose of this book is to open doors and to take you on a voyage of discovery. The everyday world around us which we take for granted is, in effect, put under the microscope for minute examination. The commonplace is made unique; the structure, the pattern, the colour of our environment is highlighted, and nothing is too ordinary to be considered as a potential subject for design. Although the chapters each deal with a different aspect they all overlap and complement one another – the same basic concepts being applicable throughout. Most of the themes are interrelated, figures can be seen in silhouette, and 'reflections' can be made on the inspiration of music and literature, so none of these subjects are relegated to watertight compartments. Design flows through all the aspects of creating a piece of work, ideas can come and go, sparking off new approaches and attitudes to embroidery.

The opening chapter explains the meaning of design, and help is given with putting your ideas down on paper. Planning, proportion, mark-making and selecting are all discussed. A shopping guide of graphic supplies is given, which lists the main requirements for drawing and designing on paper. The chapter on grids is a natural progression of the guidelines given in the above, as much of our world is based on geometric cellular structure, from plants to buildings, honeycombs to soap bubbles.

Many of us think the human figure is too daunting to use as a design source, but with the aid of Audrey MacLeod the chapter on figures sets out to help overcome some of the problems. The illustrations show various ways of depicting figures, often witty and amusing.

Coastlines, silhouettes and shadows, facades, reflections, incidentals are all considered and explored, and full rein is given to the world of our imagination in a chapter devoted to words and music. Personal preferences, memories and associations can all be brought into play. We are all individual, and the methods of recording information should be a personal process; nevertheless, a fresh approach to design will invariably be rewarding, opening up new avenues to keep work lively and exciting.

Suggestions are given for translating ideas into embroidery, and the illustrations show how artists in other fields as well as embroiderers have dealt with the various themes. In each case the individual's personal approach is evident.

We hope that the reader will gain new ideas and confidence to tackle a wider range of subjects; to gather inspiration and information with enthusiasm, and to enjoy the whole process of design from the initial stages on paper to the final project in fabric and thread.

ONE

D·E·S·I·G·N

1　Broken path study with black and white tiles (West London) 1984-5, *Boyle Family.*

Painted fibreglass 1·8 x 3·7m (6 x 12ft.). This life-size re-creation of the surfaces found in a suburban garden is a typical example of the work of the four members of the Boyle family. They choose at random a section of the earth's surface to study in intimate detail, opening our eyes to the qualities to be found in our environment.

What is design?

The Oxford English Dictionary suggests that design is a purpose, an end in view, a construction or a plot and the faculty of evolving these. Roget also adds very useful terms to guide us, like intent and composition, arrangement, grouping, balance. The roots of the word from the French 'dessiner' – to draw – and the Latin 'designare' – to specify or particularize – will perhaps help us in the understanding of the concepts involved. For the experienced artist the knowledge is instinctive and comes from many years of practice and exploration. As children we enjoy naturally the experience of assembling colours, shapes and textures, and draw without inhibition, even in the more unconventional medium of spilt liquid on a table top! Most, if not all of this, is encouraged as a form of play and means by which we can explore our environment. Why should we have to stop this exploration in adult life? We are continually making choices and decisions when we decorate a room, select our clothes, plant our gardens; many of us doodle on the telephone pad or other scraps of paper, so we are actually considering the elements of design in our everyday lives, albeit unconsciously.

Consideration of the work of artists and craftsmen can give us guidance in our own development as designers. A glimpse at the sketchbooks of such artists as Picasso shows a lifelong absorption in this visual exploration – a rearranging of shapes, lines, colours, spatial relations and so on. The artist is creating and controlling the image and not the other way round.

Formal elements

We need to consider the various formal elements that come together when we are designing. By becoming aware of these and their individual qualities we can gain greater control over the process of recording and evolving a design. Test the following list by looking at a specific object or scene, evaluate each component, noting the qualities first of all in words and then by using any of the materials and methods mentioned in this chapter.

Shape and form

The outline shape or silhouette of any object is probably the easiest to define. It is the visual reference by which we recognize much in our environment. Form is the three-dimensional version of shape, the solid as opposed to the

2   Composition 2, *Nicole* ▷
Gaulier.
   The bold linear patterns are emphasised by contrasts of tone and bright colour. This is enhanced by the change of the scale and the direction of the stripes. The design is worked in chain stitch, covering the background completely, and the result is rich and vibrant.

silhouette, and it too plays a very important part in this recognition. Outlines will vary according to where you view your subject from unless, of course, it is a perfect sphere; therefore it is necessary to gain as much information as possible about a subject by viewing it from all angles and eye-levels.

Shapes become symbols to us – a house is a box with a triangle on top – but by looking carefully at the outlines we discover that in fact one building is very different from another, one tree from another, and one person from another. The space between one shape and another is sometimes called the 'negative' shape as opposed to the 'positive' shape of the objects; both are equally important to the composition and this is demonstrated in the ingenious designs of M.C. Escher.

Line

Lines are used to describe the outline of an object or the boundaries of shapes within the object. They can become a personal shorthand to the artist as well as a way of expressing a wide range of qualities. Many artists have written about their approach to their own particular medium, and some of the most vivid comments on the qualities of line appear in the books written by Paul Klee. He spoke of line as though it were a living being with the ability to express movement, weight, space, emotion and so on.

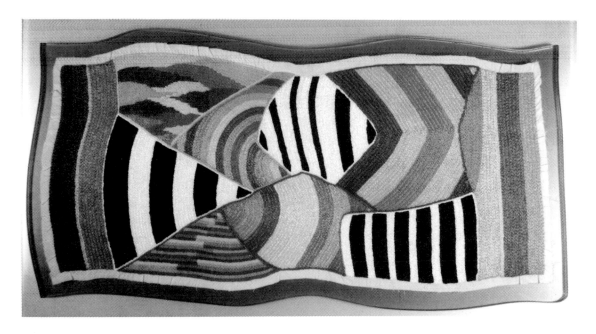

Colour

Colour can be analysed in such categories as warm or cool, dull or bright, dark or light; but also it can express mood and thus be described in the more emotive terms of strong or weak, loud or quiet, depressing or exhilarating, etc. In recent times there has been a great deal of research by psychologists into the human reaction to colour. Our response, too, is often an emotional one; some people prefer bright, vibrant qualities of pure pigments, whereas others feel happier with the subtle effect of duller, closely-toned colour or even the softness of pale, muted tints. Look carefully, too, when discovering the true colour of things: why is one green different from another, one blue from another?

Tone

Tone is an important aspect of the design process. It is related to, and yet independent of, colour, and means the degree of darkness or lightness that the eye can detect. For instance, a pure red and green can be identical in tone but are very different in colour. This relationship can be changed by darkening and lightening the original colours by adding black, white or grey. Contrasting tone can be used to accentuate a shape or part of a shape, or can be used in a more subtle manner to bring a group of shapes together to suggest one form.

Texture

The surface quality of objects is defined as 'texture', which often needs to be discovered by touching as well as looking at the surface; because of the materials used by the embroiderer this, too, becomes another important element.

Pattern

Pattern is a combination of the formal elements created by the division of a total area into a series of smaller areas, which are clearly defined by a change of tone or colour or even texture. Pattern can be used to give a complexity and richness to the simplest design, and is of particular significance to the designer of textiles.

Space

The sense of spatial depth in a design can be achieved by quite a number of devices that have been used by artists for many centuries. The great discovery of linear perspective in the Renaissance may be the most obvious and dramatic means, but the relative distances of objects from one another can be conveyed by their scale; by overlapping the forms; by the tone and intensity of colour; and even by areas of pure colour. The contradictory or ambiguous use of space can be exploited for a specific purpose, perhaps to accentuate a shape or to flatten forms into a pattern.

Movement

The feeling of movement or lack of it is an essential element in a design. It can be conveyed by the direction and quality of line, by the repetition of shape, colour or tone. Movement can, for example, be strong and dynamic; curving and swirling to create a vortex; agitated and jumpy; calm and soothing, so that a greater or lesser sense of movement is transmitted by the relationship of lines and curves, shapes and colours.

None of these formal elements is seen in isolation, and it is the interaction between shapes, colours, tones, space and movement, and textures that is the basis of design. Bringing the formal elements together can, at times, seem an overwhelming task, but practice, though it might not make us perfect, does improve our abilities in collecting, selecting, comparing, modifying, manipulating, assembling and arranging. We become more aware of ourselves and our environment. With practice we learn to balance these elements, to put more stress on one or another, so that order is created and purpose is given to our design. The value of looking at the work of artists who work in media other than textiles cannot be stressed enough, as this helps our appreciation of the use of these formal elements that are the components of the language artists use to communicate their ideas.

Materials and techniques

Sketch books

It is very useful, possibly essential, to record your impressions, whether from direct observation or from images in the mind's eye, so that a plan can be formed and a design achieved. Working in textiles, although a stimulating medium, is time-consuming; the most immediate form of recording is by using drawing or painting materials on a surface of your choice. This method is extremely flexible so that we can work as rapidly as we like, jotting down ideas almost as quickly as they come into the mind, or record carefully to give as much information as is needed. By experimenting and practising with the various media, using them separately or together, we will become more skilful and confident, and be able to pick up a pencil or pen to draw as readily as we would write.

When looking at work in galleries, note how often an artist follows a theme or an idea through many variations. The occasional opportunities to view sketch books give an even greater insight into the development of a subject from the initial ideas to finished works. Numerous examples of the evolutionary approach can be found in the work of textile artists today.

Storing information

Apart from using sketch books, it is convenient to store information in ring binders which can take a variety of papers, scraps of samples, photographs, cards, and the general odds and ends that one acquires. Plastic envelopes are useful for small items and can be added to the protective binder. Larger pieces of work can be stored in a simple folder, made from two pieces of stiff card which are taped together to form a hinge. Try to file work according to subject matter as this can save continually leafing through the work. This may seem rather painstaking, but it is worth while.

Art materials

When the painter, critic and writer John Ruskin exclaimed 'Give me some mud off a city crossing, some ochre out of a gravel pit, a little whitening and some coal dust and I will paint you a luminous picture', he could hardly have foreseen the rainbow choice of art materials in the shops today. Choose your

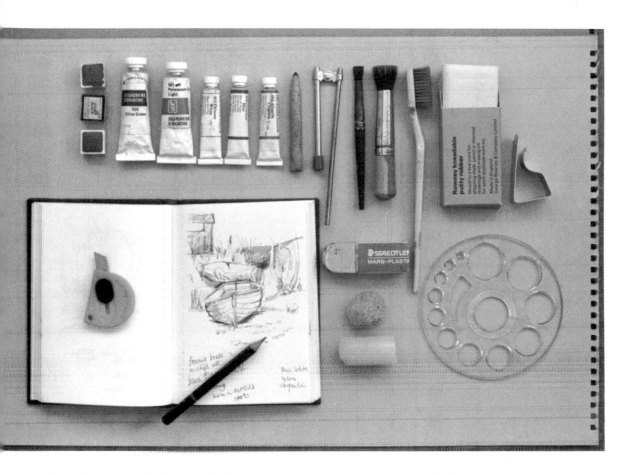

3 Design materials. (*Left to right*) *Top row:* watercolour blocks, tubes of gouache, tubes of watercolour, paper stump for pastels, mouth diffuser, stencil brushes, tooth brush, putty rubber, clip for drawing board. *Bottom row:* small sketchbook with pencil, sharpener, rubber, sponge, candle and template.

materials wisely, selecting the basics, as well as a variety to tempt the imagination. Too few, or rather, the wrong few, can be frustrating. Too many, and unity is lost and you spend time choosing instead of drawing.

Most paints, coloured pencils and crayons are available separately as well as in boxed sets. If at all possible, buy the best, especially brushes; by taking care of the equipment it will last you many years. Simplicity is also a good maxim — a soft pencil and a small sketch book in the pocket is all that is needed to make sketches at any location. Having tracked down materials that suit your needs, keep them close at hand rather than tidied away in a drawer. This way there is more chance of drawing and painting becoming an involuntary routine response to all that you see and find exciting.

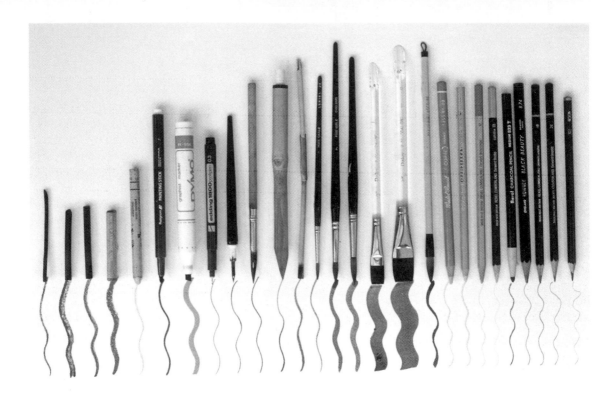

△
4   Drawing equipment. (*Left to right*): Pencils, HB, 2B, 4B, Black Beauty, charcoal, coloured, watercolour, soft coloured pastel.

Brushes – Chinese, ¾in. square end; ½in. square end; sizes 8, 7, 4.

Stick; bamboo pen; dip pen; mapping pen; drawing pen; felt chisel end marker; felt pen.

Wax crayon; soft pastel stick; Conté crayon; charcoal stick – medium and thin.

◁ 5   A rich variety of marks made on a watercolour paper, showing the potential of the mark-making equipment.
Top row: Conté, charcoal, 4B pencil.
Middle row: soft pastel smudged with paper stump, watercolour brush on wet and dry paper.
Bottom row: stencil brush, toothbrush for smudging and splattering, sponge.

Exploring design

Media and technique cannot be separated, and by exploring the use of the media a wide, rich variety of marks can be made. Try changing the pressure, spacing, direction and speed of the mark-making. The following exercises are suggested and each one will be different in result depending on the implement used, the texture of the paper and the response of the draughtsman to his subject.

Mark-making

1. Basic marks – with pencils and pens make dots, short straight lines, short curved lines, vertical, horizontal, diagonal, multi-directional; light pressure, firm pressure, varying pressure.
2. Extend exercise 1 by using Conté crayon or charcoal. These are softer and produce larger marks. Try using the point, the edge and the side to give a wide range of marks and textures. Rough-surfaced papers give interesting results.
3. Coloured chalk pastels and pencils – these can range from fine coloured pencils to thick sticks of soft pastels. Explore the marks with the use of colour, starting with limited warm/cool combinations; then extend to other colour schemes, overlaying colour to give a rich, vibrant surface.
4. Wax crayons are usually in stick form and can be used for all the exercises. Any of the crayons or pastels can create rich areas of colour if you use broken pieces on their side.
5. Apply watercolour with a variety of soft watercolour brushes. Mix a pool of colour in a small dish and try the various exercises. Keep the marks separate and be spontaneous with your brushstrokes. Let the paint dry before a second colour is used for colour experiments. Now try letting the colours run and blend, even working on damp paper. Watercolour can also be applied with a much drier brush, resulting in more textured marks.
6. Drawing ink can be applied with a brush or stick to carry out the suggested exercises. Vary the pressure as before.

Multi-media

1. Wax-resist exploits the water-repellent qualities of some crayons. Work first with the wax, which can be coloured or a white candle, then cover with a wash or marks of watercolour.

1. It is important to have a hard surface to lean on as a support – a hard-backed sketch book, a piece of plywood or a drawing board.
2. Cartridge paper is adequate for drawing but experiment with all types, including watercolour and Ingres paper, homely brown wrapping paper, newsprint, hand-made papers and other coloured papers. Collect scraps in a folder.
3. Pencils vary from H for hard to B for soft. A range from H, HB, B, 2B and 4B will be quite adequate.
4. Try a wide variety of pens, including dip pens, fountain pens and the many variations of stylus-type, fibre and ball-point.
5. Charcoal comes in both stick and pencil form, and there are a variety of colours available in Conté crayon.
6. Soft, chalky pastels come in a wide range of beautiful colours. Keep the sticks in a box with rice to cleanse them.
7. Oil pastels are rich in colour and have a greasy quality.
8. There is a good selection of coloured pencils of varying degrees of softness.
9. Coloured drawing inks have a beautiful luminous quality and can be diluted with water.
10. Collect the best watercolour brushes that you can afford; fine, medium, and large. Chinese brushes are also good value.
11. Choose your paints from the wide range of gouache colours, but try working with artists' water-colours as well for their beauty and transparency. Basic colours include ultramarine, cobalt, cadmium yellow, lemon yellow, cadmium red, and alizarin, as well as black and white.
12. A mixing palette such as an old white plate, screw-top water jars or bottles, pieces of real sponge, candlewax, pins, clips, putty rubber, rolled paper 'stumps', a craft-knife, fixative, a sketching stool, and small sketch book are all worth collecting.

2. Combine pen or pencil drawing with watercolour to give added tone and colour to the linear drawing.
3. Try the coloured chalks and crayons on different coloured papers – light, medium and dark.
4. Smudge soft pencils and pastels to blend them or extend the marks. Use a piece of cloth or tissue, a sharpened eraser or specially made paper 'stumps' from art shops.
5. Pastels worked over watercolour give a new texture and richness.
6. The introduction of metallic paints or crayons also gives a richness and contrast to the colour.

Collage, printing and rubbings

1. Paper collage is appealing as whole areas of colour, texture or pattern are placed at one time. The pieces of paper relate immediately to fabric. There is a wonderful range of papers available today, of all weights, colours and finishes, even hand-made papers, as well as the ubiquitous colour supplements and magazines. Create different edges by cutting or tearing, and assemble the collage on a firm paper or thin card back-ground using PVA glue, which dries to a clear film. The translucent qualities of thin tissue papers are enhanced when completely covered with the glue, as it dries to a glossy finish.
2. Rubbings of patterns and textures also give an immediate result which can be cut up and reassembled, worked into with paint or crayon, explored with varying colour combinations and so on. Use fairly thin paper for your rubbings and work gently at first, gradually increasing the pressure as the image emerges on the paper. Try rubbing colour over colour, even moving the paper to give a multiple image. This method is known as 'frottage', and has been used by various artists including Max Ernst, who made rubbings of floorboards and other wooden surfaces.
3. Mono-prints produce very quick images and can be made with a variety of 'printing' blocks to make solid or patterned areas of tone or colour. Mix the paint (such as poster colour or gouache) on a palette and apply fairly thickly to the block with a brush, rather than dipping it into the pool of colour. Raid the vegetable basket and try printing with sections of potatoes or turnips, which can be cut into any shapes or simple patterns. Cork or rubber also make good blocks. Using special gouges or cutters, you could even cut your own proper printing blocks from linoleum.

6 In this pen and ink sketch of ▷ riverside plants the various marks combine together to suggest and describe the form, tone, direction of growth and relationship of shapes. Areas of densely worked marks are balanced by open space. (*Vicky Lugg*)

7 Mark-making with bamboo ▷ pen, drawing pen and Chinese brush, showing the variety of marks which can be achieved by exploiting the quality of the different implements.

Improvising

Some of the more attractive drawings or paintings made are those done when we are not 'trying hard', and often with unconventional materials. It is a good idea to have a collection of odds and ends with which to experiment. Many artists use homemade reed pens or sharpened twigs for drawing. Screwed up pieces of paper, small pieces of sponge, different textured fabric can all be used for laying down areas of tone or texture. The edge of a piece of card, dipped in paint, makes excellent straight lines.

Success in these methods depends to some extent on 'touch'. Experimenting will teach you how much paint to use; often if you 'starve' the paint more textural variation will appear. You can also use your fingers to soften edges when you draw, or rub with pieces of soft cloth for delicate tones and blending. A colour-laden toothbrush scraped with a knife produces a fine splatter, which is useful for large tonal areas; you may wish to use this technique with cut or torn paper stencils. Paint or ink can also be sprayed with a mouth-diffuser.

Practical hints

- Some coloured pencils and crayons can be blended on the paper with water – this is usually mentioned on the packaging.
- Soft pencils, crayons and pastels will need 'fixing' to prevent smudging. Fixative is available from art shops.
- Try working on as many different coloured papers as possible; see the effects of light on dark, bright on dull and so on. Make the background work for you, suggesting the scene, enhancing the colours and giving the design cohesion.
- Use some of the suggested methods to create quickly broad areas of background colour for design work.

Design development

You may well ask what all this paper work has to do with textiles and embroidery, but hopefully, by working through the exercises, you will appreciate that apart from other considerations it is much quicker to try out ideas on paper than in fabric and threads. As you become more experienced the marks that you make will predict more readily the stitches and techniques that you will use in the embroidery. Marks might represent an actual stitch quality, suggesting perhaps short, spiky stitches; round lumpy ones; square chunky ones. Solid areas of colour might suggest the equivalent in fabric or closely-worked stitches. Try not to regard the designs on paper as a totally separate aspect to the work in textiles; let the two develop together as one process.

The following exercises explore a few aspects of each of the formal elements; try them individually and then in permutations, such as combining a colour exercise with one on shape. Refer to the design materials section and combine different drawing and colouring methods with your designing.

Line

1. Discover ways of expressing line without making a continuous mark, experimenting with the drawing media, for instance dots and dashes. Suggestions for textiles: translate into suitable stitches.
2. Draw a series of lines that are close together, far apart, straight, curving, jagged. Vary the width between the lines and the weight. Suggestions for textiles: Italian quilting; edges of layered fabric; stitches of varying weights.
3. Make a design with a continuous line without overlapping at any point. Suggestions for textiles: machine stitching, quilting, couching.

8   Watercolour study of trees in high summer by Sonja Head. Notice the direction of the brush marks which are highlighted with additional pastel and crayon, creating a rich and varied surface. Shapes, form and tone are thoroughly explored and recorded.

△

9　Horizontal bands of pattern traced from the original sketch are enriched with scribble-like marks in soft pencil. (*Sonja Head*)

10　A more decorative approach is made in the version with flat silhouettes and stylized shapes. Pen and pencil. (*Sonja Head*)

▽

11 Bold marks made with a thick felt pen in various densities accentuate the tone and form of the trees and the outline made by the foliage. (*Sonja Head*)

12 A reversal of tone gives emphasis to the spaces between the trees, and the simplicity of the horizontal lines shows a more abstract side of the design. (*Sonja Head*)

7

Shape and form

1. Repeat a shape in various positions to form a design, some touching, some overlapping, some filled in, some in outline. The original shape can be a template cut from card. Suggestions for textiles: stuffed shadow quilting; padded and flat appliqué, stitched background voiding the shapes.
2. Draw with a continuous line which is made to overlap on itself to produce shapes; fill these in with colour, tone, varying patterns of marks and so on. Suggestions for textiles: flat appliqué, blocks of solid stitchery.
3. Draw a simple still life showing clearly the negative shapes as well as the positive ones. Place the shapes together as you would a jigsaw puzzle. Suggestions for textiles: cut work; solid areas of machine stitchery.

Colour

1. Use the primary colours to draw grid patterns of overlaying lines and colours. Work both systematically from one primary to the next, and in a random manner too. Suggestions for textiles: couched filling stitches; machine stitching; darning.
2. Using dots of colour blend the colours of the colour-circle to move smoothly from one to the other. Suggestions for textiles: translate into stitches; canvas work.
3. Choose and record areas of colour from your surroundings varying from strong, bright colour combinations to more subtle ones. Suggestions for textiles: select equivalent threads to work small stitch samples. Use mixed threads to create colours you do not have at hand.

Tone

1. Fill in a simple design using parallel lines of varying distances apart to create the impression of gradating tones. Fill in each shape at a different angle. Suggestions for textiles: couched lines; machine quilting.
2. Translate a simple coloured picture into one of equivalent tones of black, white and greys. Suggestions for textiles: flat shadow quilting, layers of transparent fabric.
3. Repeat the same simple coloured design on white, grey and black background papers. Suggestions for textiles: stitch in one colour on varying tonal backgrounds, exploring both hand and machine stitching.

13 This design sheet by ▷ Dorothy Tucker is part of the preparation for a panel entitled 'Kite Flying at Jaipur' based on impressions of a visit to India. Drawings, photographs, fabrics and threads are brought together to give a wealth of information and stimulation.

Pattern

1. Use a simple, asymmetrical printing block to make a series of repeat patterns with the 'brick' method and 'half drop' as well as turning the block 90° and 180°. Suggestions for textiles: appliqué; reverse appliqué; inlay.
2. Assemble a design using different sizes of the same unit. The shapes can be superimposed as well as being used independently. Suggestions for textiles: flat and padded appliqué; canvas work.
3. Observe and record some of the patterns to be found in your surroundings, especially natural objects. Suggestions for textiles: solid hand or machine stitching; applied fabric and stitching.

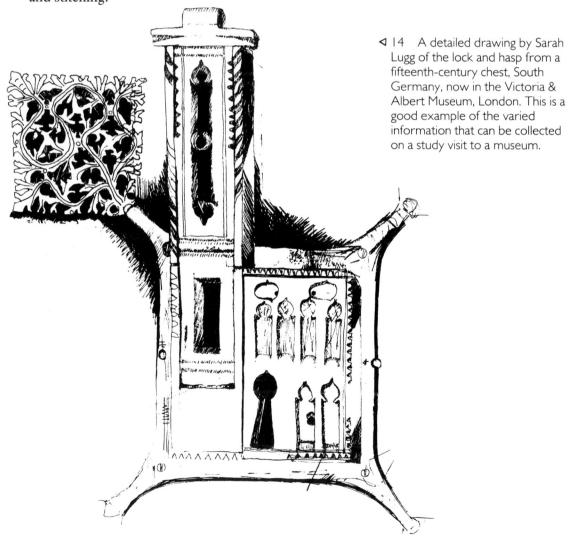

◁ 14   A detailed drawing by Sarah Lugg of the lock and hasp from a fifteenth-century chest, South Germany, now in the Victoria & Albert Museum, London. This is a good example of the varied information that can be collected on a study visit to a museum.

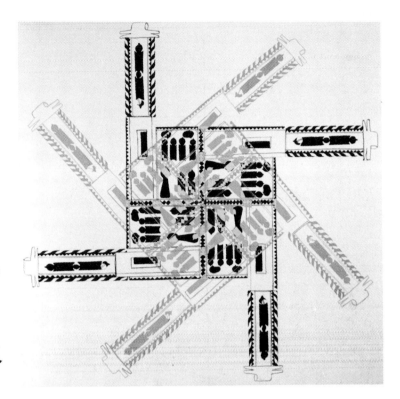

15   The outline and details of the lock are used as a repeat pattern that is overlaid to create new shapes. It was painted in flat gouache to accentuate the decorative qualities of the design. (*Sarah Lugg*)   ▷

16   A repeat pattern is evolved from the drawing of the filigree work of the hasp. The design is then developed with coloured pencils, exploring the inter-locking shapes with subtle changes of tone and intensity of line. (*Sarah Lugg*)   ▷

Texture

1. Observe, grade and record various surfaces from the very smooth to the very rough. Suggestions for textiles: hand stitching in the appropriate stitches, fabric manipulation.
2. Observe and record as many different textures from the natural world as you can, placing them together for contrast in a simple grid pattern. Suggestions for textiles: applied textured fabrics and suitable stitches.
3. Create a collage of textures using crumpled paper, card and any odds and ends that are suitable, sticking it onto a card background. Suggestions for textiles: textile collage; textured embroidery; canvas work.

17 and 18　Frozen Waterfall, *Joan Matthews*. The collage of card and paper creates exciting textures which are interpreted in a variety of threads and stitches on canvas. Note the contrast between the ribbed and tufted stitches, and the soft and shiny threads.

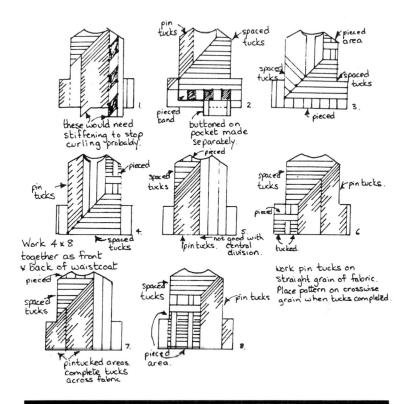

these would need stiffening to stop curling probably.   1.

pin tucks   spaced tucks   2.
pieced band   buttoned on pocket made separately.

pieced area   3.
spaced tucks   spaced tucks   pieced

pin tucks   pieced   4.
spaced tucks
Work 4 x 8 together as front & back of waistcoat

pieced   spaced tucks   5.
pin tucks.   not good with central division.

spaced tucks   pin tucks.   6.
pieced   tucked.

pieced   7.
spaced tucks
pintucked areas. complete tucks across fabric

spaced tucks   pin tucks   8.
pieced area.

Work pin tucks on straight grain of fabric. Place pattern on crosswise grain when tucks completed.

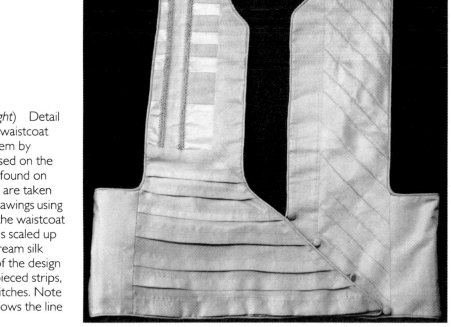

19 (*above* and 20 (*right*)   Detail of a worksheet for a waistcoat and the completed item by Christine Cooper based on the patterns of boarding found on barns. Selected areas are taken from the simplified drawings using a window cut out in the waistcoat shape. One of these is scaled up into a pattern for a cream silk waistcoat. The lines of the design are represented by pieced strips, tucks and insertion stitches. Note how the fastening follows the line of the design.

Aids to designing

A camera is very useful to record information for future reference as a back-up to your notes and drawings. It may be that the subject is moving too fast, that there is no time to make detailed drawings, or it may even be too cold to hold a pencil! Get to know the experts in your local camera shop, and take their advice on choosing the right equipment and type of film for your purpose.

Access to a photocopier can be a great help if you want to repeat a design a number of times. The photocopies can be used for cutting up and rearranging, for exploring various colour schemes and so on. Some photocopiers also have the facility of enlarging and reducing, which can be very useful.

View-finders for selecting parts of your drawings and designs are invaluable. You will find the most versatile one has a couple of L-shaped pieces of card so that the size and proportion of the frame can easily be altered. Some designers like to have a set of view-finders cut to different sizes and shapes from thin card. Shapes representing the outlines of garments, for instance a kimono, can be a great help.

Conclusion

In conclusion, choose your own approach to design, whether it is systematic or intuitive. Make the images that you choose work for you; consider the need for weight, balance, space, movement, harmony and contrast. It is succinctly summed up in the words of Aristotle 'The parts should be so connected that if any of them be transposed or taken away, the whole will be destroyed or changed, for if the presence or absence of something makes no difference, it is not part of the whole.'

21   Designs selected and traced from the plant drawing in fig. 6, using windows of various shapes and proportions.

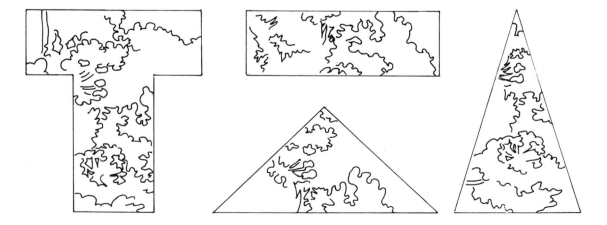

TWO

G·R·I·D·S

22   The grid structure of a lobster pot showing an interesting difference in scale as the larger framework contains a smaller netting. The natural form of the leaves contrasts with the man-made structure. (*Philip Best*)

Definition – frame of spaced parallel bars; grating; grill; gridiron; network; mesh; web; lattice; trellis; weave; lace; wicker; reticulum; plexus; network of lines; basis for map reference.

The simplest of grids can be formed by a series of parallel lines, which can then be crossed at right angles by another series. This pattern of squares can be turned at 45° to make diamonds, or overlaid by the diamonds to become octagons. A grid can be constructed from any geometric shape or combination of shapes, and beautiful examples of the rich variety of these combinations can be seen in the block patterns of North American patchwork and the tile patterns used on floors throughout the world. The simple shapes of triangles and squares can be altered into more complex forms of hexagons and octagons, and by using an increasing number of facets the straight line appears to change into a curve.

Grids can be formed by the combined use of straight and curved lines, like the barbed quatrefoils used in mediaeval design, or simply by using all curved lines. The traditional wine-glass quilting design is a perfect example of the use of the circle as a basic design component. Another lovely curved shape to use is the ogee with its sinuous balance of concave and convex lines.

In his book *Pattern Design* Lewis F. Day maintains that geometry is the basis of all pattern, and by laying an imaginary grid over even the most convoluted and complicated design this can be seen. By using this method, it is easier to see how patterns are constructed and developed; whether they are all-over repeats, border patterns, or a series which build up to make a composite design. Many artists have used grid patterns as the foundation for their work, and some of the simplest forms can be seen in the abstract paintings of Piet Mondrian. The potential of juxtaposing colour and tone within more sophisticated grids was realized in the work of Victor Vasarely. By varying the proportions of the shapes within a simple grid and using colour and tone to relate to these variations, his paintings pulsate with life. Another artist who used the distortion of a grid to immense effect was the designer Escher, and a study of his witty and inventive use of grids is very rewarding.

23   The change of scale and direction of the lines of the grid of a pylon creates a variety of interesting shapes. The overlapping of the lines in the smaller areas produces a complex pattern which contrasts well with the larger spaces. (*Philip Best*)

24   The overlapping grid of a large climbing frame creates a series of new shapes and patterns. (*Vicky Lugg*)

25   The supports of an old seaweed festooned pier are exposed at low tide, creating an unusual grid-like pattern. The overlapping shapes of the lines of the supports enhance the perspective. (*Anne Baldwin*)

26   Bamboo poles are lashed together to form the scaffolding for a high-rise building in Hong Kong. (*Michael Lugg*)

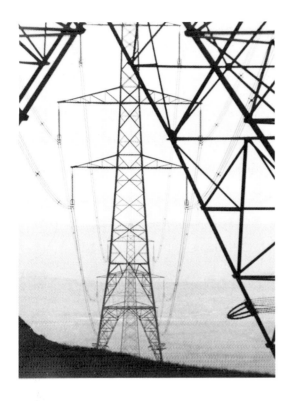

Where to look

Lewis F. Day links the development of grid patterns with the evolution of designs from the earliest Western cultures. These patterns appear in many forms and on many different surfaces. Unfortunately, owing to the impermanent nature of textiles, most of the earliest examples that we have for study are not in the form of embroidery. However, a visit to any decorative arts museum will yield a wealth of ideas for contemporary design.

A large museum or gallery can appear intimidating by its complexity and richness of content, but by narrowing down the field of investigation and directing one's attention to a specific period or form of design, this can soon be overcome. Patterns can be found on embroidered, woven and printed textiles, not forgetting those depicted in paintings. Ceramics including decorated tiles; wood and stone carvings; manuscripts; pattern books; jewellery; armour; and tableware are also sources providing design ideas. An exhibition of artefacts from a culture other than our own can surprise and delight us, giving further inspiration for embroidery.

Often these decorative motifs, which have survived throughout the centuries in different cultures all over the world, were based on religious or superstitious beliefs. Many of them were based on the nature of the materials used, in particular the geometric patterns developed directly through the technique of weaving, braiding or plaiting.

When recording information in the relatively formal environment of a museum, a small sketch book is easiest to handle for making drawings and notes. Whatever you use needs to be hard-backed to give support while you work. Make as many notes as possible so that you have adequate information for future designing. When it is impossible to make coloured sketches, written notes are very useful. Some museums and galleries allow photography, but it is always important to check first if you wish to use the photographs to back up your sketches with this additional information.

Traditional sources

Interlacing designs are found in many cultures particularly in Celtic art, and in the Hausa designs from West Africa. The interlace patterns of the Renaissance period too were used in many different scales, from the fine braid applied to clothing, to the hedges, paths and flower beds of their formal gardens. The rich complexity of both Islamic and Chinese latticework patterns are another example. The basic act of weaving,

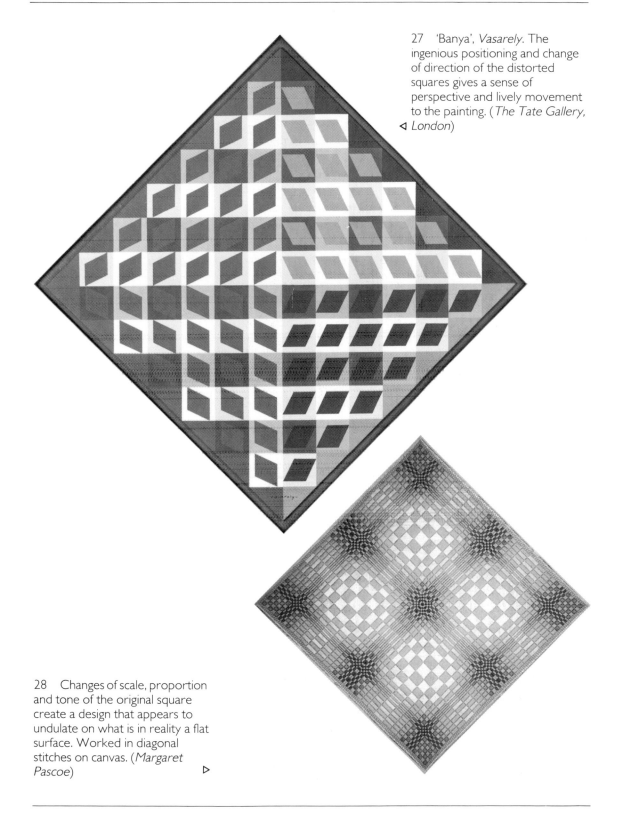

27 'Banya', *Vasarely*. The ingenious positioning and change of direction of the distorted squares gives a sense of perspective and lively movement to the painting. (*The Tate Gallery, London*) ◁

28 Changes of scale, proportion and tone of the original square create a design that appears to undulate on what is in reality a flat surface. Worked in diagonal stitches on canvas. (*Margaret Pascoe*) ▷

braiding and plaiting fibres together to create a structure has led to many beautiful and intricate designs. A wealth of inspiration can be found in the bold patterns of North African carpets, the fine quill-weaving of the North American Indians and in the beautiful and decorative articles from the Far East and throughout all the world.

Man's environment

Many of the materials that man has used in building and decorating his environment throughout the centuries create the most fascinating grid patterns. Building materials such as bricks, stone, tiles, preformed concrete blocks, girders and scaffolding are just a few examples. Decorative tiles and mosaics are used on many surfaces. The structure or framework of buildings, the doors and doorways, windows and glazing bars, surface detail on the walls, are all elements which form their own network of pattern, varying from stark simplicity to florid decoration.

The underlying structure of railings, wrought ironwork, fences and trelliswork which form barriers is based on a simple grid, as are wire baskets, fishermen's nets, vegetable nets and crates.

Grids in nature

Plant growth patterns form grids of both a formal and informal character. The regular spiral patterns of pineapple skins, fir cones and many flower heads can be taken out of context and developed into surface design. In contrast to this the random grids formed by criss-crossed stems and branches can be equally adaptable.

Incidental grids

Much of life today is dominated by systems and programmed patterns, which create their own formal grids. The possibilities of using modern technology are endless; for example, computers replace the drawing board for designing graphic layouts for advertising, as well as exploring the permutations of colour and pattern for woven woollen cloth. Accidental grids are often formed when objects are stacked together.

Grids are also apparent in the aerial views of anything from field systems and urban streets to the simple grid of a games board, which in turn is used for the more complex grid pattern of the game played on it.

Developing a design

Grid patterns lend themselves readily to design because of their beautiful simplicity. The structure gives obvious guidelines to a design and provides an easy starting point for the less experienced. The simplicity can lead to complexity and, as in Islamic art, very rich and elaborate designs and patterns can be created. The geometric and formal nature of grids as a starting point can also be adapted and developed into informal and apparently spontaneous designs. The following suggestions for development can be combined and adapted at will.

1. Experiment with the combination of various geometric forms, which can be made easier if graph paper or isometric paper is used. Variations of the simplest designs can be made with colour, tone, texture and pattern. Try using cut-up photographs, photocopies of textures, patterned wrapping paper and so on to fill in the shapes.
2. Replace some or all of the original straight lines with curved lines.

29 'The Corridor', *Vieira da Silva*. A great sense of perspective leading the eye to the end of the 'corridor' is cleverly contrived by the changing scale to the chequered grids. There is also a feeling of light and movement which adds to the interest of this very individual painting. (*The Tate Gallery*)

◁ 30   Tile Pattern, *Mary Fortune*. Squares of random-dyed fabric are pieced together to form the centre of a small cushion. The symmetrical, scrolling design is quilted in a fine back stitch using a random-dyed thread.

△
31   Part of a fifteenth-century tile pattern from the collection in the British Museum, London. The complete pattern is painted over sixteen square tiles, and is the basis for the design of the quilted cushion.

3. Vary the thickness of the structural lines, giving consideration to the relation of the lines and the shapes they contain.
4. Cut up drawings, photographs or photocopies or a combination of these into strips and reassemble or weave them together. The strips can be of equal or varying widths, and the spaces between the reassembled pieces can also vary. Try placing the weavings on different coloured backgrounds, considering the effects of colour upon colour and tone upon tone.
5. Cut a drawing, photograph or photocopy into squares, rectangles or other geometric shapes, and experiment both by moving these shapes slightly apart or rearranging them. As before, experiment with the spaces between the shapes, and the colour and tone of the background on which they are placed. This method could be used for more random shapes, perhaps in particular to the starting points of windows, nets, railings, trellis, plant stems, etc.
6. Stencils cut in the form of a window with the pattern of glazing bars can be used to place over drawings and photographs to achieve interesting results.

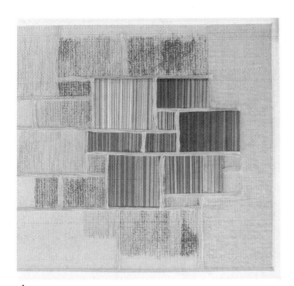

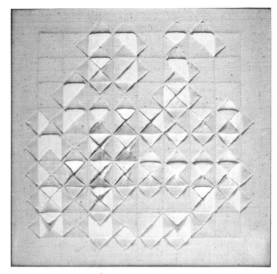

△
32   The irregular grid of a stone
wall inspired this experimental
study by Lesley Barnett. Thread-
wrapped card is superimposed
on a pastel drawing.

△
34   'Calico Squares', *Vicky Lugg*.
Layers of calico and cream silk are
machined together in a regular
grid pattern. In some areas the
layers are cut through to create a
random design within the grid.

△
33   Purse, *Muriel Best*. The
design is based on a distorted grid.
The patchwork effect is achieved
by using a variety of stitches,
including trellis, laidwork and
satin, which is also raised over a
base of thick vilene.

△
35   'Knot Garden', *Vicky Lugg*. A
small panel featuring an interlaced
design applied to a background of
sprayed fabric, and enriched with
surface stitches, especially french
knots.

36 'The Trellis', *Vicky Lugg*. The informality of the free stitching in a variety of threads is contrasted with the more formal pattern of counted stitches and applied ribbons. The small panel is worked on canvas, painted to blend with the embroidery.

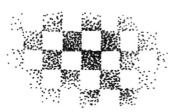

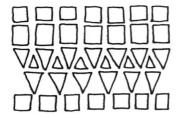

7. Lay a grid pattern over the top of a drawing or design and develop the colours, tones or patterns of the drawing using a counter-change method.

8. Try laying grid over grid, shifting the alignment slightly so that new shapes are formed and new grids created.

9. Experiment with the contrast of scale by changing the size but keeping the same character of the unit, also by placing small grids within large grids. Other variations could be to use a single unit in a regular and irregular pattern, and to use part of the unit as well as the whole.

10. Grids can be distorted and change form within the one design, as can be seen in the work of Escher and Vasarely. The distortion of perspective is exciting to use and wonderful three-dimensional effects can be explored with the use of colour and tone.

11. The change of the grid structure can also be made to follow a mathematical formula. The artists of the Renaissance used a grid based on the Golden Mean in their compositions. Other formulae include the Fibonacci series of numbers and many more which are based on the work by the earliest mathematicians.

12. Many ideas of combining formal grids with informal shapes can be found in oriental art. Often a number of different grid patterns are used within one large design. We can learn much about surface design by studying the subtle use of straight and curved lines in all aspects of oriental art.

37 Examples of a few grid variations on the basic square grid.

Interpretations

The immediate relationship of grids to the actual structure of the background materials used for embroidery is obvious, and lends itself to most of the techniques that are the inheritance of the modern embroiderer. The suggestions for both design developments and interpretations are worth cross-referencing to give innumerable, exciting and innovative effects.

1. Counted thread techniques relate immediately to grid designs, especially canvaswork. Try experimenting with large-scale canvas, wrapping the structure with machined satin stitch or hand-winding threads or strips of fabric. This produces a rich background that can then be embellished still further. The counted surface stitchery used in blackwork, Wessex stitchery and pattern-darning are excellent starting points, as well as the regular grid-like effects that are formed by decorative filling stitches, for

38   These drawings are based on one of the many systems of numbers devised by the Italian mathematician Fibonacci after his careful study of Islamic art. This particular system is based on the series 1; 2; 3; 5; 8; 13; 21 and so on – the new number is the sum of the previous two numbers.

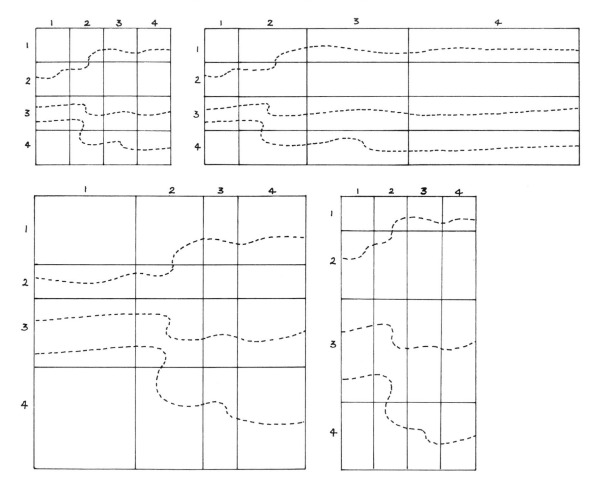

39   Coarse cotton lace is based on a square mesh structure accentuated in this drawing by the shading of the spaces between the threads. (*Vicky Lugg*)

40   The simple square grid of a woven check pattern is distorted as the fabric is draped and folded. (*Vicky Lugg*)

41   Layers of grids are apparent when coarse net curtaining material is folded against itself. (*Vicky Lugg*)

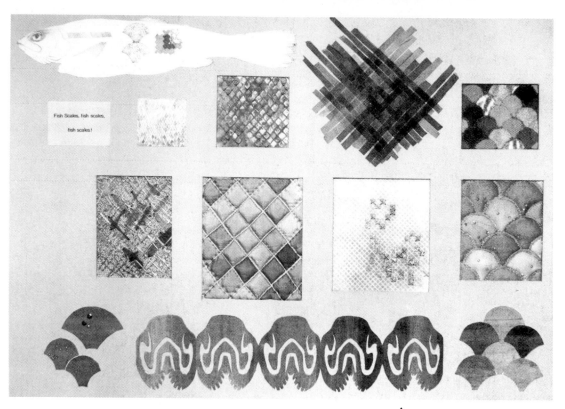

△

42 'Fish Scales', *Clem Gelder*. A worksheet exploring the pattern of scales, from working with paint, strips of coloured paper woven to form a grid, through to small experiments in fabric using quilting, patchwork, and hand and machine embroidery.

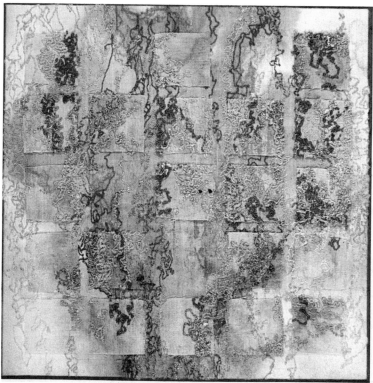

◁ 43 In this sample by Mary Fortune, painted fabric decorated with machine embroidery is cut into squares and rearranged onto a toning embroidered background. These are blended together with further machining.

example couched filling, chevron filling and fly filling. Experiment freely with colour, weight and texture of thread; with the scale of the stitch and the space between the stitches, working both formally and informally.

2. Patchwork is also an obvious technique to use, and there are many superb examples of the traditional designs. To experiment by designing and cutting your own templates, and combining patchwork with methods of surface decoration would develop this tradition still further.

3. Techniques that explore the possibilities of altering the surface of the fabric such as smocking and quilting have great potential. The actual method of smocking forms its own grid-like pattern, which can be as formal or informal as you please. Try experimenting with unusual fabrics, like plastics, felt or leather. Quilting in all its variations acts as an excellent interpretation of grid designs, especially when

44 Window at Brighton Pavilion, *Christina Gale*. The machined glazing bars are silhouetted against the darker areas of layered silky fabric which form the glass.

both straight and curved lines are used. Distorted, diminishing shapes, lines that curve and interlace, grids that change scale and form – all these can be interpreted in both plain and shadow quilting.

4. The designs created with woven paper can be interpreted immediately into fabric, with an interesting use of texture or colour or both. Try using rouleaux, torn strips, folded strips and embroidered strips for this exercise. An impression of these designs can be created with the use of running stitch, working with a variety of threads including strips of fabric.

5. Embroidered fabric can be cut up and rearranged to create the same effects as the paper designs. Hand embroidery needs to be firm or fixed at the back with a light gluing. Machine embroidery will adapt particularly well to this method.

6. Machine embroidery – with the foot on; the nature of the line achieved with both straight and zig-zag stitches lends itself with great ease to the creation of grid patterns. Exciting effects can be achieved with unusual fabrics, like plastic and hand-made paper, also by layering fabric, quilting and so on. Machining over textured surfaces, like those created by Italian quilting or tucking, gives an exciting richness by rearranging the fabric, and giving fullness.

Free machining can be used to fill in geometric shapes and the experimentation with fabrics and threads can be particularly rewarding in this area of design. For example, blocks of closely-worked machine stitching on felt or velvet create exciting contrasts with the unworked areas. The use of dissolvable fabrics is equally effective, but of course, totally different in result. Fine, web-like structures based on grids machined onto these fabrics can be used as a separate entity or applied to a background.

7. Many of the above techniques, especially the more traditional ones, can be extended by using random-dyed fabric and thread, giving a delightful informality to the more formal work of drawn and counted thread.

8. The incorporation of fabric paints opens up a wide variety of new approaches. Paints that are sprayed through stencils or printed onto the fabric relate immediately to the grid designs created originally on paper. Transfer paints have great versatility as the paper onto which they are painted can be cut up and rearranged before the colour is ironed off on to the fabric. Lightly glue the rearranged, painted, paper pieces onto a new sheet of paper to control the pattern during the ironing process.

45   Detail of grid patterns in a doorway of Brighton Pavilion. (*Muriel Best*)

THREE

F·A·C·A·D·E·S

46   Contrasting textures of the various materials used to mend the wall of an old shed. The details of the nail heads and cut and frayed edges add to the total effect. (*Philip Best*)

Definition – the face of a building towards the street; open space; front; forefront; proscenium; face; fascia; mask; falseness; make-believe; affectation; semblance; masquerade.

A facade is the front or appearance presented to the world, an exterior which may or may not reflect what is really behind it. The expression 'a mere facade' is commonly used, implying that an object is not a true representation but a mask or false front.

For the purpose of design the term facade can be interpreted in many different ways. The fronts or outward appearances of buildings provide a wealth of ideas, from Tudor houses with their geometric patterns of beams, and Regency houses with their elegant proportions, decorative ironwork balconies and moulded pilasters to modern glass-sided skyscrapers. Quite apart from the general lines of the buildings the very texture of the materials used is attractive, particularly to those who work with textiles. Smooth stone in mellow tones, rough plaster, wattle and daub, flint, brick, timber and lichen-covered tiles all have their own appeal. Neglected buildings with peeling paint and crumbling walls are often more interesting to study closely than those which are carefully maintained to present an immaculate image to the world. The ancient and crumbling city of Venice is a case in point. The beautiful old palaces and houses reflected in the waters of the canals, and the lovely faded colours have inspired many artists, notably Turner who captured superbly the wonderful quality of light over the water.

However, facade can also mean the front that an individual presents to the world. Indeed, the clothes we wear are in a sense a facade, and we choose them to suit particular occasions. The rare occasion of a fancy dress party gives the opportunity to hide the true self behind the character portrayed. Even the shyest person may be tempted to be quite outrageous if they can hide behind a mask, at least until midnight as tradition dictates. A clown whose aim is to make people laugh often conceals a serious and melancholy personality beneath his smiling mask and bizarre costume. In the world of opera the characters often change places, hide behind their assumed identities and arrange clandestine meetings; nobody is what they seem, and usually everything ends in confusion.

47 Detail of an old crumbling wall showing joss sticks in their holders. Smooth and rough textures, and the fragmented shapes make an interesting surface. (*Sarah Lugg*)

48 The jumble of objects that accumulate around working and living areas in downtown Macao. A cobweb of electricity cables festoons the buildings. The clothes hanging up, and the piled pipes together with assorted machinery give a fascinating insight into what lies behind the facade. (*Michael Lugg*)

49 A glimpse behind the facade of a building. Note the old carved doorway of this building which is in the Barbican area of Plymouth, Devon. (*Philip Best*)

50 An air-conditioning fan set into the window of an old Chinese house makes an interesting set of shapes not unlike a piece of modern sculpture. (*Michael Lugg*)

Where to look

Why not begin by going outside to look at your own home? Notice the texture of the walls, the pattern of the tiles on the roof, the design of the windows, the eaves and any ornamentation on the brickwork over the doors. You may be quite surprised to discover the design possibilities in something which hitherto has been taken for granted or gone unnoticed.

Having studied your own home, look around at the other buildings; notice how the windows differ one from another – some may be made of leaded glass with tiny panes set in a lattice framework, others may be large panes with louvred panels at the top. Roofs differ, and the styles vary: red curved tiles are common in parts of Yorkshire while slate tiles are popular in Wales and Cornwall. Thatched cottages provide another interesting source of patterns, and the way of tying the thatch changes from county to county. Climbing plants like wisteria, ivy and rambling roses all provide additional colour and texture.

In an urban environment the walls of buildings can be encrusted with posters and graffiti. Torn posters with fragments of letters making disjointed messages can be the starting point for a fascinating design. Peeling paint, splashes of colour, broken fences and derelict shells of buildings are all there waiting to be discovered and translated into terms of fabric and thread by the embroiderer. On a train journey one of the most interesting parts can be from the outer suburbs to the inner city. The panoramic view of the seemingly identical rows of houses is enlivened by the touches of individuality shown in the colours chosen for paintwork, and the appearance of the gardens. Some will be neat and well-cared for, others sadly neglected. In the city itself tall office blocks, hotels, churches and historical buildings all jostle together in a conglommeration of assorted shapes and sizes.

So much for the exterior of buildings – let us look now at another aspect of facades, the world of masquerades. The colourful scene of the Mardi Gras, the extravagant, bizarre costumes and masks could be translated into a design for a lively embroidery, full of movement and colour. The ancient Japanese heroic Nō dramas make great use of masks and sumptuous costumes. The actors wear masks symbolic of the characters they are playing; fans too, are an important accessory and play a vital part in all the stylized gesture of the drama.

Slate

Straw Thatch

Reed Thatch

Thatched Barn

Pantiles

△

51   Sketch book drawings of roofs, showing the patterns of different styles of thatching, and of different types of tiles. (*Muriel Best*)

52   Machined and stiffened strips of fabric are moulded over tubes to simulate a pantile roof. (*Bernadette Wright*) ▽

53   Loosely woven scrim is frayed and fringed to create this impression of a thatched roof. Stitches act as spars to keep the threads in place. (*Bernadette Wright*) ▽

◁ 54   Worn blocks of sandstone
are the inspiration for these
padded shapes covered with
knitted and machine-
embroidered fabrics. (*Jean Rocke*)

55   Beads made from rolled
paper, fabric and suede are
stitched to a textured background
material which is derived from a
pebble-dash facade (*Judith
Newell-Price*)

△
56   Line drawings showing the
construction of a stone wall. The
interest is created by the varying
sizes and shapes of the individual
stones. (*Hilary Williams*)

◁ 57   The broken tiles of an old
barn are re-created using
machine stitches on painted
paper, giving a patina of colour
and texture. (*Jean Rocke*)

Developing a design

As you will see from the illustrations much can be made from the details of buildings, whether it is the repeating pattern of roof tiles, the stepped design of bricks or the rough knobbly texture of pebble dash. The ornamentation of plaster on an Edwardian house provides the inspiration for one embroiderer who uses quilting and cut layers of fabric to achieve her effects. Try out some ideas using the following exercises as starting points.

58 Brick infills on a timber-framed building are stitched in fine canvas work and applied to a background. (*Jean Rocke*) ▷

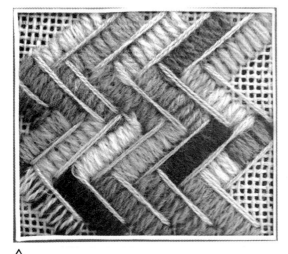

△
59 Tapestry wool gives a very different texture from silk. Long stitches suggest the mortar and accentuate the herringbone pattern. (*Judith Newell-Price*)

△
60 Random-dyed thick silk yarn on canvas recreates the subtle tones and colours of old bricks. (*Judith Newell-Price*)

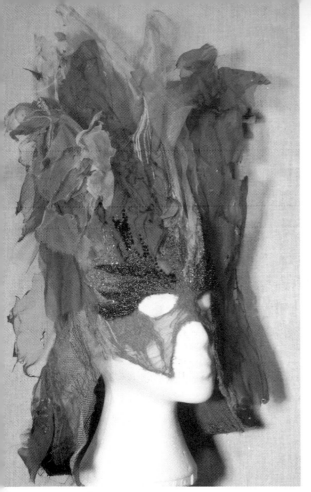

61 This imaginative combination of mask and headress by Elise Lynch is inspired by fire. The stiffened gauzes are torn and stitched to represent the leaping flames. The detailed stitching in metal thread is concentrated around the eyes.

62 Machine embroidery in a variety of threads, textures and patterns stresses the dramatic quality of this design based on a Japanese mask. Metallic paper is used under some of the stitching to give extra sparkle. (*Jane Walter; The Embroiderers' Guild Collection*)

◁ 63 Wooden masks used for Japanese Nō performance (*left to right*): Otobite – a devil in human form; a woodcutter or fisherman; and Mambi – a bewitching woman. (*Muriel Best*)

52

△
64   The model at the start of the
make-up session, with guide lines
drawn across the features for the
black and white mask.

△
66   The make-up used as a mask
totally disguises the face, and the
dramatic black and white design
creates a sinister air of mystery.

△
65   In Japanese style, with the
eyes accentuated and the hair
piled high.

△
67   Au naturel – the model as
herself. The series shows how the
appearance of one person can be
altered to present a completely
different facade to the world.
Model, *Sarah Lugg*. Make-up, *Jane
Rivers*. Photography, *Antony Best*.

1. Use mixed media (paper, fabric, stitching, paint, etc.) to make a collage giving the effect of a crumbling surface. Fragments of paper printed with letters will add interest. Look at the collages made by the artist, Kurt Schwitters. He used all kinds of paper, from newsprint to tickets, pieces of string, washers, anything which he felt was an interesting shape or texture, to build up his collages which he termed Merz.

2. Another exercise might be to imagine that you have been asked to design and make a decorative mask for a character in an opera, ballet or pantomime. Colour and detail can be exaggerated to enhance the effect – a splendid opportunity to indulge in 'flights of fancy'.

68   Two masks that would give an air of excitement and mystery to their wearers. (*Left*) Machine embroidery and delicate fabrics by Shirley Crawford and (*right*) corded and stiffened fabric, machine-whipped stitch, by Sheila Gray.

69   Collage by the German artist Kurt Schwitters, entitled 'Opened by Customs', which typifies his use of collected scraps of paper, including wrapping and newspaper with added paint and drawing. Note the contrast of the surfaces thus created. (*The Tate Gallery, London*)

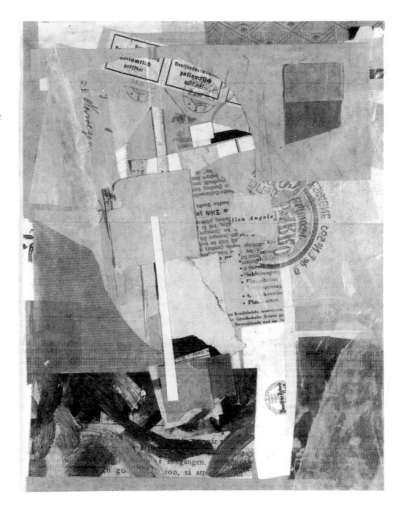

One of the first things to determine when designing the mask is the size. Is it to be a full face or one which goes across the upper half of the face only? If it is to cover the face completely the fastenings must be efficient and comfortable; a half mask could in fact be held to the face by means of a suitably decorative stick or baton, which would be attached to one side.

3. Look around you and note how many different surfaces you can see on walls; make notes and record them using some of the methods given in the chapter on design.

◁ 70 Drawing of a detail of the decorative moulding. (*Joan Matthews*)

◁ 71 An interpretation of the drawing worked in English quilting on a white silk fabric. (*Joan Matthews*)

72 Part of the relief decoration from the facade is interpreted in layers of calico, hand stitched together to give a sculptural effect. (*Joan Matthews*)

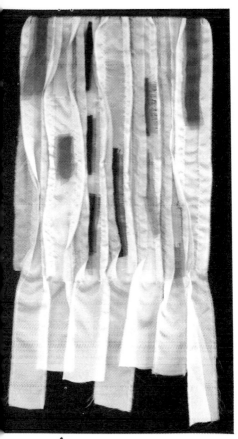

△

75 Torn posters provide the inspiration for a series of experiments; the first is a collage of torn and cut paper giving an interesting layered effect. (*Joan Matthews*)

76 The third example again exploits the quality of torn, frayed and burnt edges using fabrics of different textures. The shadows of the overlapping edges add to the effect. (*Joan Matthews*) ▽

74 The second example is worked in transparent fabrics, ripped into narrow strips and assembled with machine stitching to repeat the layered look. (*Joan Matthews*)

◁ 73 The front of an Edwardian house, which has decorative moulding over the door and windows, in the form of a vine and flowers. (*Joan Matthews*)

Interpretations

The variety of surfaces and textures which we have observed in the facades of buildings can easily be translated into terms of fabric and thread. The choice of materials available to the embroiderer corresponds in a sense to those used by the builder.

1. Develop a panel or hanging from your collage, perhaps using ripped fabric to suggest the torn posters and crumbling surfaces. Try to make a feature of the disjointed lettering using a smooth fabric or flat stitching to contrast with the rough texture of the other surfaces.

2. Having designed a mask the next step is to decide on the method of construction. It is possible to buy plain masks which are usually made of papier maché, alternatively it is quite simple to make your own. A polystyrene wig stand is also very useful as a former on which to build your mask. Small pieces of transparent fabric joined together by machining can be used to build up the shape. The pieces could be assembled on dissolvable fabric, for ease of handling while machining, and finally moulded into shape. Rich fabrics, beads, wrapped threads, metal threads and ribbons can all be used to create the character of the mask.

3. From your observations of different surfaces make small experiments perhaps using layers of fabric, pleating, tucking, folding and quilting to obtain a variety of different effects.

77 A row of houses in a country town showing the different periods of architecture. The patterns on the Tudor buildings contrast with the simplicity of the Georgian ones. (*Muriel Best*)

FOUR

F·I·G·U·R·E·S

78   A group of figures patiently waiting for a ferry on Macao. (*Michael Lugg*)

Definition – External form; bodily shape; representation of the human figure; statue; physique; torso.

In the words of the artist Audrey MacLeod:

'Many of us find drawing the human form difficult and challenging, even attempting to describe the process leads us into a labyrinth of complexity, for we are all too aware of the standards set in classical antiquity which continue to provide us with canons of beauty that have rarely been surpassed. For many of us the artists of the high renaissance in Italy – Michelangelo, Leonardo da Vinci and Raphael – represent the apotheosis of human achievement in expressing the perfection of the human form.

In the Protestant northern countries, prolific artists such as Dürer showed us the rigorous discipline of draughtmanship, whilst the English court was sufficiently dazzled by Holbein's delicately-drawn portraits to commission likenesses of most of its members. But of the Flemish masters, although charmed by Ruben's flamboyant cherubs tumbling about the ceilings of chiaroscuro clouds, it is the humanity of Rembrandt that truly warms us. Rembrandt's rich portrayal of the family bond and heroic myth and biblical narrative is the superlative expression of the human state.

The following pages show different ways of approaching figure drawing by a variety of artists from the Greek vase painters of the early sixth century BC to the innovators of the mid-twentieth century.

We know and see so much that has been done with perfection that we feel bound by tradition and artistically impotent. It takes courage to pick up a brush and start to paint. Yet the great artists began in much the same spirit as we do, with an awesome appraisal of what is before us coupled with the struggle to understand.'

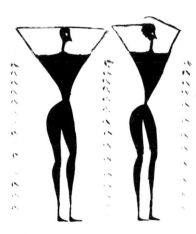

Where to look

Perhaps the most obvious way of observing the human figure is to look around at your own environment – people at work or play, shopping, gardening, reading, walking, running, jumping, sitting, standing and kneeling. Notice the difference between a figure in action and one that is still and relaxed. Movements can be jerky and tense or flowing and graceful; but the standing figure must have a centre of balance, flowing from the neck downwards to the feet – without this it will fall over. If one leg is raised from the ground, the balance will shift to the other one, so that the heel of the foot is directly in line with the neck. Try standing on one leg in front of a long mirror and observe the shift of balance.

Groups of figures provide interesting over-lapping shapes and patterns, for instance heads and shoulders packed in rows at the theatre, or crowds watching a tennis match, their heads turning from side to side in unison. Think of the precision of a troupe of tap-dancers, and the rigid straight lines of soldiers on parade, their uniforms emphasizing the areas of pattern.

△

79-81   The silhouetted figures ▷ are from the Dipylon amphora *c.* 750BC and belong to the geometric period of Greek art. Subjects were seafaring depictions, charioteers and the 'prothesis' or lying in state of the dead, from which these figures were taken. Mourners are shown in the traditional lamentation pose with their arms above their heads. They are simplified with frontal views alternating with profile views of forms and limbs. (*Audrey MacLeod*)

82 'Playground', *Wendy Lees*. The figures of the children in a playground create ever-changing shapes as they group and re-group in their games and activities. Notice the shapes that are created between the figures and shadows. Sprayed paint and straight stitches on a background of silk noile.

Footballers and rugby players provide plenty of action, with their movements at times seeming almost balletic as they leap from the ground.

The French artist Degas drew and painted ballet dancers as they really are, both on and off the stage, rehearsing, putting on their shoes, resting and relaxing. Toulouse-Lautrec portrayed the singers, the dancers and the audience at the *Folies Bergère* with tremendous vitality and economy of line. Look at the work of artists and sculptors, look at photographs in magazines and newspapers, from fashion models to scuffling demonstrators – are the figures relaxed, graceful, poised, elegant, tense, distorted?

Often stylized symbols are used to represent figures – the signs in effect becoming an international language. This approach is useful for the designer, a device to use when realism is unnecessary and the pattern-making qualities need to be emphasized. The painter T.S. Lowry often filled his scenes with small matchstick-like figures which nevertheless have great vitality and movement. Now having looked, the time has come to put your observations down on paper.

Getting started

Audrey MacLeod gives the following guidelines . . .

'When we draw, three things come into play: the subject, our response to it and the materials and techniques used to express this response. In front of the model we act as a sensitive "filter"; a receiver of perceptions which we attempt to put down on paper. There are some basic rules, but ultimately the response has to be a personal one.

It is a good idea to discover the qualities and limitations of our drawing materials before starting, as they have a life and will of their own. Once we begin drawing we will be too taken up with finding the essential lines of the pose, constructing forms and simplifying shapes, to worry about techniques. The human body is geared for high performance and action. Like a machine it is "sprung" to take stresses and strains, to alternate between tension and relaxation. We can try to express this action with speed and energy. Sometimes it helps to experience the movement before we start to draw. Limber up; feel the tensions of the pose then our lines will echo the action we feel. They too will dance; the brush will bounce. The paint can, and probably will run, smudge and drip. Spend some time looking and observing the characteristics of the pose. Feel your way into the drawing by starting vaguely and letting the lines grow on the paper. Work from the general to the particular and back to the general, making sure before laying down your pencil that you have expressed the initial ideas about the pose.

To help loosen up before you commence a "long pose" make some rapid sketches from the model; it encourages quick thinking and the grasping of essential lines and shapes. Progressive movement poses are also testing, and the ballet class is a good subject. Overlay the sequence of movement as it changes, using different weights of line or different colours to prevent a confusion of shapes. When drawing the figure we can express it in terms of line, shape, structure, movement and proportion.'

◁ 83 'Dancer Looking at the Sole of her Right Foot', *Edgar Degas*. Bronze sculpture. Notice the position of the body over the left foot giving balance and stability to the figure. (*The Tate Gallery, London*)

84 Drawings in soft pastel show ▷ a dancer moving through the sequence of an exercise. The overlapping lines of each pose give a sense of gentle, flowing movement. (*Sonja Head*)

◁ 85   The vigorous quality that charcoal gives to a drawing is typified in this study of figures in action by Mary Foreman. Lines are redrawn and tonal areas quickly established with this medium.

Techniques for drawing the figure

Audrey continues . . .

'The fear of the stark white paper is common enough: "white fright" is the usual term for it, and it can be overcome in various ways.

1. Sketch in the shape of the head and the central supporting line of the pose and mark in the feet. A good approach is to draw lightly at first as you will find you need to make continual adjustments. Place the main directional lines of the pose in relation to the central line and the axis of the shoulder line and hips. Include lines of support such as chairlegs and add lines of the floor and wall to give you more guidelines and shapes.

2. Draw in the forms, reducing them to their most approximate geometric shape. Look for the spaces between forms and construct these in the same way.

3. Assess the proportion and scale of the parts to the whole and to each other. Measure distances and mark off in a system of dots or small vertical and horizontal lines. Lines and marks describe action through their movement and placing rather like a shorthand system. Go for the dynamic action and life in a line, and your marks will be expressive and forceful. Lines can be rhythmic, slow, fast, energetic or lethargic. Lines can hop, run, bend, shrink, grow, jump, jerk or dance.

4. Simplify all the shapes, contrasting large with small. Look for the shapes outside the figure as well as inside. Find the main contour lines of the pose. Look for clues to help you, especially in the way drapery follows the form in the clothed model. Describe form with directional hatching, variation of line and blocks of shading.

86 Rapid brush drawings using ink and a Chinese brush on calligraphy paper, by Mary Foreman. This type of brush is held vertically onto the paper and the drawings are made very quickly.

▽

Now try drawing more than one figure. Find a crowd. Take out a small sketch pad and felt-tipped pens, and find a place with lots of activity – a playground, swimming pool or gymnasium. Draw the directional lines of people moving. Try not to look at your hand as it draws. Make a number of quick sketches, notice how a group of people compress together to make one shape and then move apart in isolation. How have your lines behaved? Do they grow fainter and smaller in the distance? Are they heavier when they advance towards you in the foreground? Try to set the scene with whatever is around – ducks, deckchairs, people's clothing – to give an indication of the environment.

◁ 87 'Sumō Wrestlers', *Sue Ribbans*, in padded and applied shapes. The entwined bodies of the protagonists create abstract patterns against the background of the wrestling mat, relieved by the fiercely human expressions on their faces.

Developing a design

One of the best ways to use your figure drawings as a basis for design is to think through your figure studies again in terms of a new medium. Do not try to reproduce a sketch exactly. Designing comes with the process: the doing and the undoing! One way of experimenting with shape for design is to use the method of cut or torn paper. At the end of his life Matisse, the great French artist, was constantly inventing and improvising by this method. His statements about the technique are as simple and as fresh as his ideas. He described "papier decoupé" and "dechiré" (cut and torn paper) as "drawing with scissors".

88 'The Model', *Joy Real*. Paint, appliqué and surface stitchery combine together to present a charming picture of a model with a parasol. A great deal is expressed with the minimum amount of fabric and thread. ▷

◁ 89 'Madame' *Joy Real.* This delightful portrait of an old lady pouring milk into a bottle is built up with applied scraps of plain and patterned fabric – machine embroidered to give added colour, texture and pattern.

90 'Pearly Queen with her ▷ Granddaughter', *Kate Lynch.* The entire surface of the picture is covered with machine embroidery in fine threads, creating the contours of the faces and the patterns on the clothing, carpet and wallpaper. Notice the flat, stylized shapes of the figures. (*Embroiderers' Guild Collection*)

91 'The Orchestra', *Sonja Head.* There is a sympathetic use of tone and stitch pattern in this blackwork interpretation of a group of young people making music together. The geometric lines of the background contrast with the more rounded shapes of the heads and bodies.

▽

1. The following exercise is based on the method used by Matisse:

(a) Paint some areas of paper in brightly coloured (pure, not mixed) gouaches. Make no attempt to match the colours exactly and let the brush marks show. The paint can vary from the opaque to the transparent.

   Matisse used deep and light Japanese green, emerald green, deep cadmium yellow and red, yellow ochre, deep Persian orange, red and violet. These coloured shapes were cut out and tentatively arranged against a background of ivory white.

(b) The direction of the brushmarks, tonal and colour variation and the different qualities of tearing and cutting will all contribute to the final result.

(c) Do not attempt to 'cut out all in one piece'. Build up the forms gradually, limb by limb, overlapping at will. If you leave gaps between the forms and shapes like a white drawing line the eye will scan and complete the sequence of forms.

(d) Relate the scale of the shape to the paper size. Move the shapes about, considering the overall placement of pose and the balance of positive and negative shapes. Matisse placed small dabs of glue to set his shapes on the background support.'

2. The following exercise is based on tracing and overlapping shapes:

Using a tracing paper, select areas of your drawings which give a variety of shape and contour. Isolate one area and experiment with outlines, overlapping, and turning the paper to make a repeating pattern. Complicated drawings can be simplified by tracing the most dominant lines, or by using either the horizontal or the vertical lines. One figure can be traced and retraced until it is duplicated many times, overlapping at spaced intervals to produce a pattern similar in effect to the lines on moiré silk.

   Instead of using the complete figure, try concentrating on just one aspect. In his painting *Walking Dream with a Four Foot Clamp*, the American artist Jim Dine shows pairs of legs, all wearing different shoes, silhouetted against the background. The repeated shapes of the legs make an interesting pattern, as does the witty and observant three-dimensional embroidery by Shirley Crawford, illustrated in this Chapter. The identical legs of the chorus line, stepping out in the best Hollywood

92   A drawing of a seated figure is traced and repeated to make an interesting pattern of overlapping shapes, which could be the basis for a design, with some areas filled in with solid stitching, colour or tone. (*Muriel Best and Vicky Lugg*)

△
93 'On Your Bike', *Sonja Head*.
The ingenious use of horizontal
straight stitch in a variety of tones
and colours gives movement and
speed to this picture of racing
cyclists. This is enhanced by the
lack of detail and the placing of the
figures within the narrow shape.

musical tradition, make their impact by repetition.

3. Eye designs:

Eyes have often been used in art as symbols. On the top of the
Buddhist stupa in Kathmandu, the eyes of Lord Buddha are
painted on all four sides to look out unblinkingly at the world.
In Ancient Egypt eyes were considered to be the most
important feature of the face. The eye of the god was
reproduced on amulets and worn as a charm to guard against
sterility. Eye make-up was part of the daily toilette for women;
the eyes were outlined with kohl, and green malachite powder
was used to shade the lids. Eyebrows too were emphasized with
the browline drawn arching down onto the cheekbone.

Make a design which uses the eye motif as a repeat pattern.
Look at the stylised treatment of the eye in the art of the ancient
Near East. In eye make-up today the eyes are often
accentuated for dramatic effect, and this too could be used in
the context of design.

4. Using an artists' lay-figure:

The artists' lay-figure made of wood, with jointed limbs and
moveable head and torso, is useful for working out various
positions of the body in action; to see just what is and is not
feasible. If a wooden lay-figure is not available, it is quite easy
to construct one in thin card. The joints can be made to move
by attaching the limbs together with a two-pronged metal tab,
of the kind used for holding papers together.

△
94   A collage of legs and feet to be used as a starting point for an embroidery design. The idea is based on a painting of walking legs by the American artist, Jim Dine.

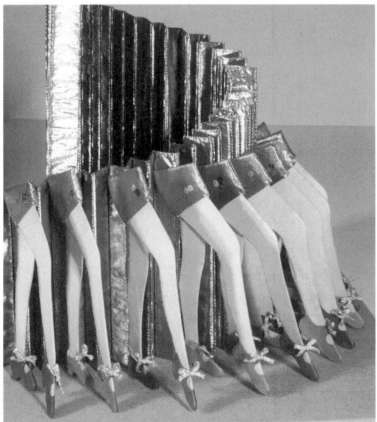

◁ 95   'Chorus Line', *Shirley Crawford*. A nostalgic and amusing interpretation of the glamorous legs of the girls tap-dancing their way through a Hollywood musical. The card-covered legs are attached to the folding background which is self-supporting.

96 'Speakers' Corner', *Sue Lackie*. The machine-embroidered and
quilted calico audience crowd around the central figure of the speaker.
This three-dimensional piece clearly shows the ever-changing pattern
that can be obtained from the overlapping shapes. The flat silhouettes
of the crowd are in contrast with the rounded figure of the speaker,
creating interesting outlines of heads and shoulders, legs and feet.

◁ 97 'The Three Graces', *Patricia Sales*, is a charming pastiche based on Rubens' painting of the classical subject of the three sister goddesses in whom beauty was deified. The figures are built up individually on a painted background with additional surface stitchery.

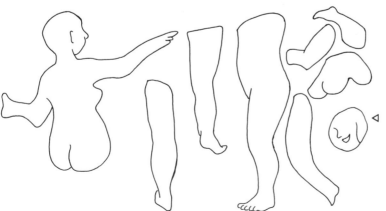

◁ 98 Templates for the figures of 'The Three Graces' showing how the layers are built up. The pattern shapes for the figures are cut out in card and then covered with wadding and fine stretch fabric. (*Patricia Sales*)

99 'Flower of Wales', *Margaret* ▷
McDowell. These two delightful
rugby supporters proudly
wearing their country's colours
are portrayed in padded and
raised work. The faces, hands and
feet are made from modelling
clay, and then painted. The
scarves and hats are worked in
detached buttonhole stitch, as is
the 'Flower of Wales'.

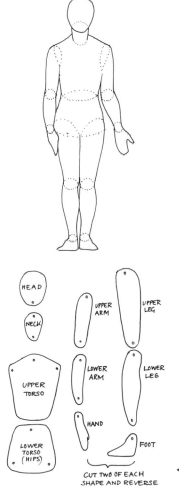

HEAD

NECK

UPPER
ARM

UPPER
LEG

UPPER
TORSO

LOWER
ARM

LOWER
LEG

HAND

FOOT

LOWER
TORSO
(HIPS)

CUT TWO OF EACH
SHAPE AND REVERSE

CUT OUT IN THIN CARD,
ATTACH BODY AND LIMBS
TOGETHER AS MARKED
BY USING A FLEXIBLE,
SPLIT PIN OF THE KIND
USED FOR HOLDING PAPERS
TOGETHER

◁ 100 and 101 Assembling a
lay-figure from thin card, to be
used as a guide for constructing
figures. The parts are moveable
so that the figure can be put into
various poses.

Interpretations

As can be seen from the illustrations the human form and its component parts can be interpreted in many ways, reflecting both actions and emotions. So many embroidery techniques are appropriate, and here are a few suggestions.

1. Designs using cut paper easily translate into fabric. Large areas of fabric can be tacked down to represent the main shapes and worked into with stitches. The design could also be built up from numerous small pieces of fabric in the manner of a mosaic, and then held in place with hand or machine stitching.

2. Stylized shapes can be used to construct a figure (use the lay-figure as a guide) in thin card which is then covered with fabric; pad with wadding if you wish. Stretchy fabrics are the easiest to use as they can be manipulated round the curved shapes. Build the figures onto a background or use them in a free-standing manner to develop a three-dimensional construction.

102   A study sheet of eyes, *Muriel Best*, showing many interpretations of the subject. Studies of the eye and its various components are combined with coloured drawings recording how the eye was observed in previous centuries and cultures.

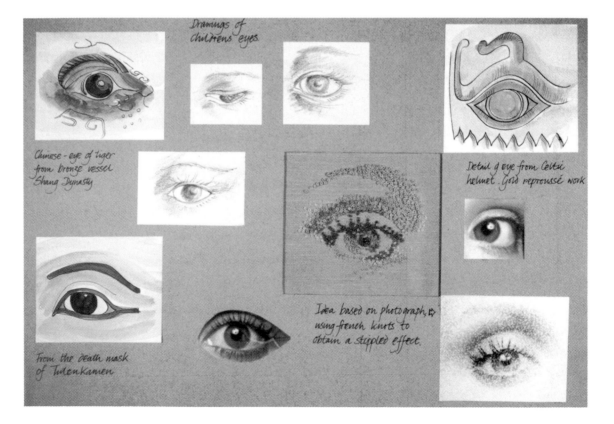

103   Little Hannah', *Joan Smith*.
There is a charm and freshness in
this portrait of a beloved
granddaughter playing in a
summer meadow. A variety of
stitches including cretan are
worked in fine threads on a
painted background.

3. From your study of eyes and the patterns you have developed think how they might be used as a decoration on a garment, perhaps forming a border or a yoke. The stylised motifs lend themselves well to cut work or appliqué; concentrate on the interesting curves and shapes eliminating minute detail. Even though your design was originally based on an eye the finished result should be an abstraction removed from reality; avoid an 'eye-ball to eye-ball confrontation'!

The work of the embroiderers illustrated shows a variety of approaches to representing the figure, clothed and unclothed. Sometimes a single figure is assembled by the over-laying of scraps of fabric, which is then decorated with machine embroidery, and others are padded and raised from the surface. In each case the result is based on careful observation with, in some instances, a witty and humorous 'tongue in cheek' interpretation.

104   Line drawing of an artists' model which contrasts the simple outline of the body, with the patterns of the surrounding fabrics. (*Sarah Lugg*)

FIVE

S·I·L·H·O·U·E·T·T·E·S

105   Two figures silhouetted against an open window create an
evocative picture. (*Antony Best*)

Definition – the portrait of a person in profile showing only the outline, all inside the outline being usually black on a white ground; the appearance of a person or object seen against the light so that the outline only is distinguishable.

The dictionary definition of the word 'silhouette' is derived from the name of the Minister of Finance in France under Louis XV, a M. Etienne de Silhouette. His hobby was to cut out paper profiles of people, and thus the term 'silhouette' came into the language. Other profilists were John Miers and Josiah Wedgwood, who used the profile relief to decorate his china. One of the methods used to obtain the outline was to sit the model between a screen and a light and then trace off the shadow. Cutting profile portraits out of black paper was a very popular pastime in the Georgian and Regency era, at both professional and amateur level.

Profiles and shadows are inextricably linked, and there are many examples in both Eastern and Western art of their use as decorative motifs, and as a basis for the expression of deep-felt beliefs and superstitions. There was, and is, a strong conviction in many cultures that the shadow represents the soul and much good and bad fortune is attached to this belief. To have the shadow of a certain person fall across you could be a portent of trouble or to walk on someone else's could also bode ill. The interest in symbolism of shadows is delightfully illustrated in the story of Peter Pan and his great concern over the loss of his shadow!

Shadow puppets have been used for story telling throughout the world; sometimes they were made with complicated cut-out images. Some puppets today are made from metal, as in the East Indies, and can be made to perform the most intricate gestures and actions. In Japan, shadow plays are performed by actors working behind a screen with lighting behind them.

106   The variety of sizes and shapes of plants on a window-sill are integrated by seeing them in dark silhouette against the light. This has the effect of eliminating the detail and emphasizes the pattern-making qualities. (*Vicky Lugg*)

107 'Check Mate', a plate from A. Edouart's 'Treatise in Silhouette Likenesses', 1835. The cut paper images are set against the drawn background of the room. (*Victoria & Albert Museum, London*)

CHECK MATE.

Where to look

It is interesting to study how the silhouette has been used by numerous cultures over many centuries. Early man was able to transmit graphically silhouette-type drawings, and this still remains an immediate form of communication and information. Greek and Egyptian potters decorated their vases and amphorae with magnificent examples of silhouettes. Any flat pattern is in fact a silhouette – for example, simple block printing with something as unsophisticated as a cut potato. This creates strong bold images with an emphasis on the positive/negative aspect of design. Apart from experimenting with this form of pattern-making, it is worth researching in both museums and libraries.

In our own environment we are aware of many silhouettes and shadows every day of our lives. Any direct lighting will cast shadows; objects against the light appear in outline form. When you look through windows an image is formed by the frame, the glazing bars, edges of blinds or pelmets, objects on the window-sill, even the pattern of net curtains. A skyline in any environment is exciting – whether the filigree branches of trees on the horizon or the complexity of roof-tops and buildings in an urban setting. Look around at the different shapes of roofs, spires of churches, chimney pots, gable ends, masts and aerials.

The appearance of the environment can depend so much on the time of day and the quality of light. When the sun is low on the horizon the outline of the landscape is accentuated and the

△

108 'View from Hawkwood',
Vicky Lugg. A pen and wash
impression of a distant landscape
seen beyond the shadows and
silhouettes of the trees and fence.
The dark tone links the various
component parts of the scene.

109 The brightly lit sky reduces
the skyline of the buildings into
one long continuous shape,
accentuating the angles of the
roofs and the details of the
chimneys, posts and trees. This is
enclosed by the horizontal shapes
of the foreground. (*Muriel Best*) ▽

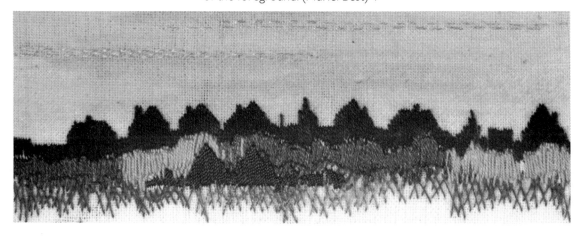

110 A series of silhouettes are created in this panel by Pauline Mackenzie, linked by the grid of the leaded window. Included is the silhouette of trees reflected in the glass and the dark area of the pelmet behind the window. Layers of fabric, including silver leather and transparent gauzes, are machined stitched and cut away.

details of the trees, buildings, fences and hedges are lost in the shadows. However, look for the subtle nuances of tone and colour that can still suggest the scene; this is particularly true of the evening light, when the rich beauty of the setting sun has such a special quality. This can be enhanced by the patterns of the clouds in the sky, which at times appear to be a continuation of the landscape as line after line of silhouettes can be seen. These views are at times enhanced still further by the appearance of ground mist in both the evening and early

◁ 111   Tissue paper is an excellent medium for designing as it is slightly translucent. Layers of black, grey and white paper are used for this landscape. (*Bobby Riddle*)

◁ 112   Layers of torn net are overlapped to create the impression of a misty landscape. The tones are carefully graded to give the illusion of space and distance, and this is accentuated by the machine-stitched trees in the foreground. (*Bobby Riddle*)

113   The overlapping iron-work of the Eiffel Tower creates an intricate pattern of grids. (*Antony Best*)   ▷

114   A delicate tracery of   ▷ silhouettes is created by the branches, leaves and flower heads of a sumac tree. The oriental quality is reminiscent of the simplified shapes seen in Japanese woodcuts. (*Vicky Lugg*)

mornings. The scene can take on the mysterious quality of an oriental print with the grey outlines of hills, trees and hedges emerging from the soft pale lakes of mist. The diffused light of a rainy day can produce unusual designs as the silhouettes of shapes appear to come and go in the changing scene to give quite dramatic effects.

Another altogether different situation, this time as a result of stronger, more direct light, is the pattern created by groups of objects all contained and linked by the shadow of a larger object. This could be a group of figures sitting and standing in the shade of a tree or verandah. The shadow flows across the forms joining them into one outline. On a more intimate note the view through a window often contains objects seen in silhouette. This again, of course, relies on the intensity and balance of the light. You need to be looking into light to achieve this effect, just like the original silhouette artists. Try creating your own arrangement of objects, plants, etc., as well as looking for more impromptu 'still lifes' on other peoples' window sills. Plants and leaves round the window on the outside create another series of shapes to add to the design. A drawn blind or curtain enhances the air of mystery, especially if figures are added to the scene creating their own shadow-play.

Developing a design

To see shapes in silhouette or shadow can simplify even the most complicated forms and eliminate any details – it is this simplicity which is worth exploring and evolving in your search for designs. You are reliant on the quality and direction of light in the general environment, but it is worth experimenting with set pieces in your immediate surroundings. A simple still-life containing a number of varying shapes can be lit with directional light to achieve some exciting and unusual results.

Observe the shadows that are formed, especially if the light is from more than one direction, as is the case in the illustration of Eileen Hogan's work. Try distorting the surface of paper or fabric on which the shadows are falling, either by pleating, folding or crumpling it, and look at the new images that are formed. The shadows can be lengthened or shortened to exaggerate them, according to the angle of the light source. All these observations can provide excellent starting points as you are practically designing with the light.

115 'Window at Hawkwood', ▷ *Margaret Rivers*, shows an ingenious use of sprayed paint combined with surface stitchery. Various stencils are used to mask relevant areas of the background, and the stitches are confined to delineating the window and describing the vase of dried twigs.

Silhouettes and shadows rely heavily on the use of tone, the ultimate being the exploitation of the extremes of black and white. Colour becomes very low key and unimportant, though it is interesting to explore the use of colour against colour as well as tone against tone. Try to discover the colour of shadows. Many painters have exploited the dramatic qualities of light, including Rembrandt, who used dark mysterious shadows to emphasize the story he was portraying. The Impressionists took up the theme, for example in Monet's studies of haystacks the shadows are rich and resonant with violets and blues.

Many of your previous design experiments could be used for this particular section, so try incorporating them with the following suggestions:

1. Working on a dark-toned paper, develop the 'negative' or background shapes of a simple design of your choice, with tone, texture or pattern leaving the 'positive' shapes as silhouettes. Suit the marks that you make to your subject – for example, a group of figures in a garden, in an imaginary scene, or even purely abstract shapes.

116 'City Skyline', *Bobby Riddle*. Applied transparent fabrics are built up to create the dark tones of the buildings against the lighter sky. The background is lightly painted and the details are machine-stitched in metallic threads to show the lighted windows. ▷

2. Try recording your information on silhouettes by using tones of grey paper, plus black and white if necessary. Tissue paper is particularly useful as it can be overlaid to create yet more tones. Tear and cut the paper to give a variety of edges, and work into this with pastel or charcoal.

3. Simplify shapes by cutting stencils and templates for use with sprayed or splattered black paint or ink. Move the shapes around between spraying, keeping them separate or overlapping as you wish, to achieve multiple images, being careful not to smudge the wet paint.

4. Shapes can be developed into silhouettes by tracing off their outlines and using closely-toned dark colours in this outline to contrast against a lighter background.

5. Ink blots have been used as starting points by many artists, in particular the eighteenth-century painter Alexander Cozens. Make blots at random by dropping or splattering ink or paint onto paper, trying the effect of dark on light and light on dark. These can be developed by blowing the wet ink or paint to form new shapes and runnels, which might suggest unexpected designs and patterns. Try extending these further by drawing into them with pens, brushes and even pieces of stick.

◁ 117 The silhouette of the fence against the light-toned meadow is a reversal of the outlines of the trees in the background. The dark tones under the trees lead you into the mysterious depth of the wood. (*Vicky Lugg*)

118 A design sheet by Sonja ▷ Head shows how the selected shapes from the photograph are developed and simplified into the final design. Various alternatives are chosen and discarded, using the drawing medium to suggest tonal areas and textures. The embroidery is worked entirely in straight stitch.

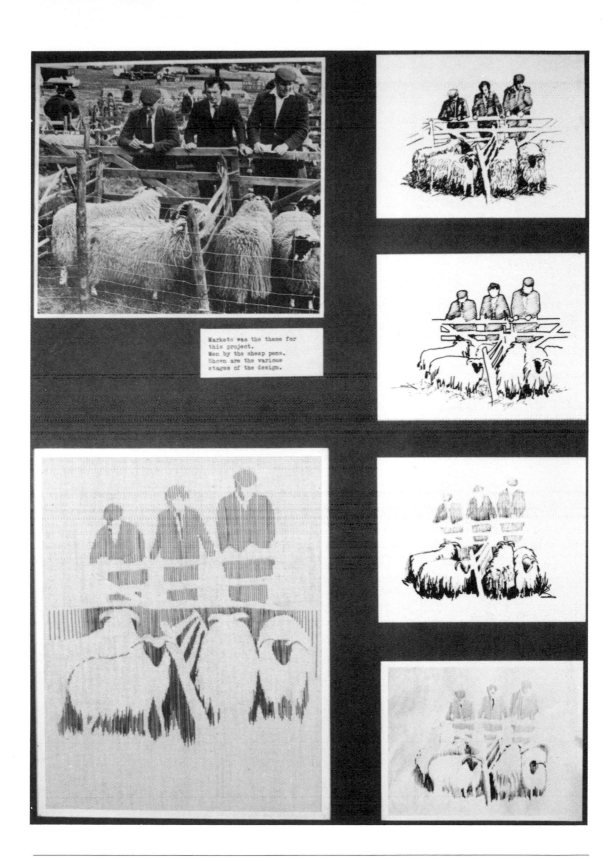

Markets was the theme for
this project.
Men by the sheep pens.
Shown are the various
stages of the design.

119 A detail from Brighton Pavilion (*Christina Gale*) uses pulled work to suggest the tracery of the architecture.

120 The pattern created by the pots on a balustrade is repeated with fabric paint on a semi-transparent fabric. (*Jo Routs*)

121 The Children on the Shore (*Muriel Best*) is worked mainly in straight stitch on a semi-transparent fabric.

122 'Male Dancer', *Wendy Lees*. The silhouette grows out of the shadows cast on the floor making a dramatic image against the background lighting.

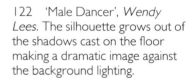

123   Figures seen against the
light merge with their long
shadows cast by the winter sun
low in the sky. (*Vicky Lugg*)
▽

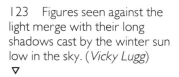

△
124   'Le Vitrail Rose', *Rosemary
Campbell*. A detail from an
embroidery of a Parisian
cemetery. The design is worked
in shadow work in a free way to
vary the tones and shapes of the
shadows and silhouettes.

125 Torn and frayed transparent fabrics are used with great effect by Margaret Rivers in this shadowy landscape. Pattern and detail are given with the painted foreground and frayed edges.

126 Trailing plants worked in shadow stitchery on organdie are mounted on a painted and machine-stitched background, echoing the plants as they are silhouetted against a window. The herringbone stitches are worked in both dark and light threads. (*Jo Routs*)

127   The shadow of a potted palm on a balcony creates an intricate pattern on both the wall and the floor. Notice how this pattern is distorted by the angle of the wall. (*Vicky Lugg*)

128   The outline of the flowers, stems and leaves of a plant are silhouetted against a background of shading. The individual shapes link together to make larger, composite shapes and the shading emphasises the negative in-between shapes. (*Muriel Best*)

Interpretations

1. Perhaps the most obvious interpretation of silhouettes and shadows is to use transparent fabric to build up layers of tone. Choose one of the designs you have made in paper and translate this into the equivalent fabrics. Explore the possibilities of tonal changes by layering the fabrics in varying combinations, cutting, tearing and fraying the edges to give different effects.

2. Shadow work on transparent fabric would give a direct interpretation of shadows cast by an object. The pattern of light and dark created by the fronds of the potted palm in the illustration on page 95 would be perfect for this technique. Try using a variety of threads of the same tone and colour, varying the density when making the herring-bone stitch to give a change of emphasis.

3. The designs and the stencils from exercise three can be used for spraying directly onto fabric, for instance for a set of cushions. Use a special fabric paint for this project that is colour-fast. The sprayed shapes can be quilted or decorated with surface stitchery.

4. Using your 'blot' designs as a starting point, exploit the negative or background shapes. Fill in the background with stitches, increasing their density round the shapes to sharpen the outline of the silhouette.

129 The Manhattan skyline at sunset. The various shapes and heights of the New York skyscrapers seen in the distance merge together in a tranquil silhouette, belying the frenetic bustle of the city. (*Muriel Best*)
▽

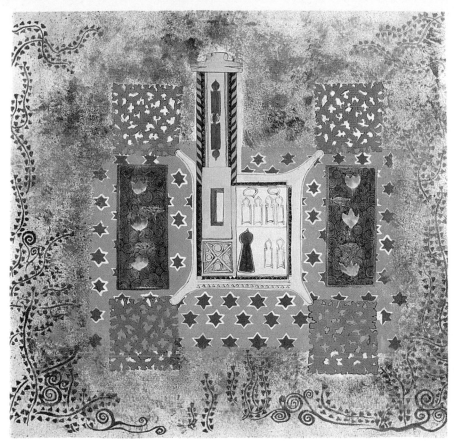

△

1　Design developed from drawings of an ornamental lock. The filigree effect of the pierced metal suggests a decorative quality which is developed in the background patterns. Gouache on paper with gold used to highlight the soft and subtle colour scheme. (*Sarah Lugg*)

2　'Kaleidoscope'. The simple ▷ grid pattern of squares is developed into a greater complexity by using interacting lines of rich colour. The straight stitches of silk thread are worked on canvas, which is covered with green silk gauze with a central area of pink lurex. (*Vicky Lugg*)

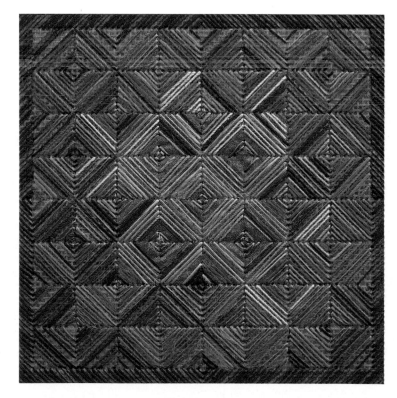

△
3   'City Lights'. The interaction of the complementary colours of purple and yellow is used effectively in this quilted silk hanging. The impression of counter-change is the result of masking and spray-dying the fabric. Shiny fabrics and threads add to the incandescent impression. (*Bobby Riddle*)

4   'West Wall at Ely'. The ▷ overlaying of fabrics and nets builds up a rich and sensitive image which re-creates the atmosphere of the beautiful mediaeval building. Hand stitchery gives added detail and structure to the washes of colour, emphasising the patterns of the facade. (*Esther Grainger*)

ELY·WEST·WALL·

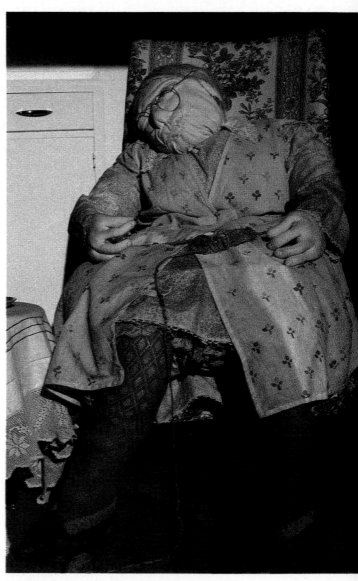

7 'Naxos Taverna', watercolour ▷
of an area of the southern
Peloponnese in Greece. The
painting by artist Eileen Hogan
emphasizes the play of light and
shadow which creates intricate
patterns from the legs of the
tables and chairs in the taverna.

△
5   The facade of carnival-time is
created in this make-up with all
the elements of make-believe and
fantasy. Sequins and ribbons add
to the effect. Model, *Sarah Lugg*,
make-up, *Jane Rivers*.

6   'Granny'. This life-size figure is ▷
constructed and clothed mainly in
calico, with stretchy fabrics used
for the head, hands and legs. The
patterns on the clothing are
printed with fabric paint to fit in
with the faded monochrome
colour scheme. The fabric of the
face is manipulated and stitched to
create a memorable personality.
(*Patricia Sales*)

8   Reflections of boats in the water of a harbour are fragmented and reassembled into intricate abstract patterns not unlike a modern painting. The interplay of the subtle colours created by light and shadow adds to the interest. (*Antony Best*)

▽

◁ 9 The old door to a fisherman's hut makes a fascinating study. Peeling paint in a crazed pattern of lines, tarpaulin crumbling away showing a grid structure on the backing and the old padlock all add up to a varied and interesting surface whose colour and texture give many possibilities for design. (*Philip Best*)

10 'Disco'. The flashing disco ▷ lights and strong rhythms of 'pop' music are the basis for this embroidery. Large sequins, metallic paper, ribbons and strips of fabric are used with simple stitchery to create the effect of a 'disco'. Muriel Best.

◁ 11 'Chronochromine $^1 2\!/_4$'. Helen Pincus is a singer as well as an embroiderer, and her work is greatly influenced by her love of music, using rhythms and emotions as a starting point. Wrapping metal rods with strips of raw-edged fabric as well as threads is just one of the techniques that she uses. This piece is one of a set of twelve panels which can be assembled and re-assembled in a variety of permutations. The fabric used is a richly printed silk. (Photograph *Clive Stirling*)

△

12 'Hope – Colour Sound Series'. In this richly coloured assemblage on rug canvas many different elements are combined to produce a vibrant and exciting image. Around the edge the canvas is painted and stitched with fabric and threads. The centre is created with layers of fabric and stitchery as well as the application of paint, small plastic toys, buttons and beads. (*Julia Caprara*)

SIX

R·E·F·L·E·C·T·I·O·N·S

130   Surface ripples distort and fragment the reflections in the water of a harbour scene. (*Antony Best*)

Definition – contemplation; reflected light or colour; an image in a mirror; a turning, bending or folding aside.

The theme of reflections can be construed in many ways, but perhaps the most immediate to come to mind is of an image which is mirrored in another surface. Buildings and trees by a river bank which are reflected in the water are obvious examples. On a still day the surface of the water will be like glass, and the image will be an almost perfect replica; however, if the wind blows, a bird lands, or a fish jumps the surface will be disturbed and ripples will spread, distorting the reflection.

Boats bobbing about in the water will have distorted reflections that can form incredible, intricate patterns of swirling shapes making fascinating abstract designs. The light shining on the water, high-lighting the ripples and waves makes further patterns, and the low setting sun mirrored in the sea creates an impression of liquid gold. After heavy rain the puddles left behind act as mirrors for their surroundings, drops and drips from trees breaking up their surfaces.

Looking glass mirrors reflecting the image of a person or the interior of a room are a source of more ideas. The domed glass of convex mirrors curve the image whilst also making it smaller, a device which Anthony Green the painter has used in his work. A visit to the 'Hall of Mirrors' at a funfair will provide the most distorted reflections, making people look either grotesquely fat and squat, or incredibly tall and thin. Mirrors have featured in many stories and superstitions; to break one is said to bring seven years' bad luck. In the fairytale of Snow White, the wicked step-mother looks into her magic mirror and asks, 'Mirror, mirror on the wall, who is the fairest of them all?', expecting to see herself, but instead seeing Snow White. In *Alice through the Looking Glass* by Lewis Carroll, Alice steps through the mirror to a magical dream world.

Modern buildings with great walls of glass reflect fractured images on different panes. A large office block will sometimes reflect the old buildings of the town in its windows, presenting an incongruous contrast of ancient and modern. Clouds reflected in these glass-sided buildings alongside the sky itself give rise to surrealistic effects, not unlike those seen in the paintings of Magritte. Metallic surfaces reflect their surroundings: a silver teapot mirrors the objects nearby, making a whole room appear in miniature. Shiny foil balloons, too, give a myriad of incredible reflections.

131   A distorted reflection of one building in the large glass windows of another. The image is broken up and straight lines become curved. (*Antony Best*)
▽

132   The outside, inside. The car outside the building is reflected in the small window giving the impression that it is on the inside. The size, height and shape of the window have the effect of telescoping the objects reflected. (*Muriel Best*)   ▷

133   A glass bowl filled with dried flower heads makes interesting patterns and gives the illusion of rippling water. (*Muriel Best*)   ▷

134   In one of the greenhouses at Kew Gardens giant waterlily leaves float on the surface of the pond, in which the structure of the building and the people are reflected. (*Muriel Best*)   ▷

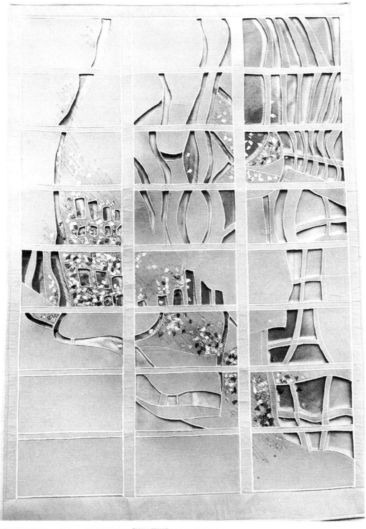

◁ 135   'Reflections', *Moyra McNeill.* Machine cutwork and appliqué are used to interpret the abstracted images of reflections in a window.

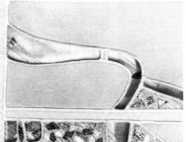
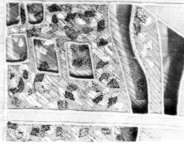

◁ 136   Detail of the embroidery showing the second layer underneath the holes of the cutwork.

△
138 'Waggoners' Wells'.
Watercolour by Vicky Lugg. The
direction of the brush strokes
suggests the smooth, satin-like
surface of the water.

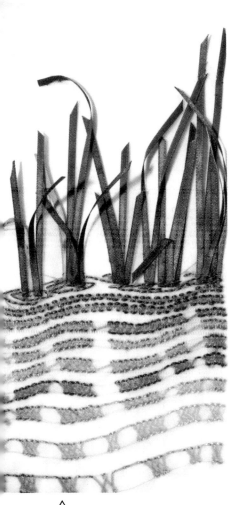

△
137 Reeds growing along the
river bank are reflected in the
ripples of the flowing water. Note
how the reflections are developed
in the gently curving lines of
varying widths and intensity. The
shadow work accentuates the
transparent quality of the water.
(*Joan Matthews*)

Where to look

Begin by looking around the room you are in and note how
many reflecting surfaces there are and what they reflect. The
greater the curve of the surface, the more distorted the image
will appear; while silver will act like a mirror, glass, especially
moulded or cut glass, will reflect more abstract patterns and
shapes. Now go outside and look into the room through the
window; the light will reflect what is behind you onto the glass,
giving a complicated montage of shapes and objects. A
photograph taken looking into the room from outside will often
give a surrealistic picture with ghost-like images. A person
sitting in a chair in the room can appear to be partly inside and
partly outside in the garden, with the photographer also visible.

Rain drops or dew on plants reflect a miniature world in the same way as a convex mirror; a photograph can be taken with the droplet in focus and the surroundings out of focus. This effect could provide a starting point for a design. Write a list of all the possibilities, take photographs and make drawings of all those which seem to have the most potential for an interesting design. The trunks of trees and their network of branches reflected in water are a typical example, with perhaps the reflection distorted by the ripples. Exaggerate this aspect by making the trunks very straight and the reflected image curving.

139   The interior of a cave with stalactites reflected in a pool. Simple canvas work stitches are used to good effect, contrasting formal straight lines with the broken irregular lines which depict the rippling reflection. (*Joan Matthews*)

140   The patterns of marbling on fine silk form the basis for this panel by Rosemary Caie. The upper half is developed with hand and machine embroidery accentuating the shapes, tones and colour. The addition of small beads gives areas of texture to the general smoothness of the piece.

Developing a design

If you decide to develop a design from the broken, fragmented images in glass-sided buildings, simplify the shapes and use the window frames as a grid. Concentrate on the pattern qualities and try out several ideas using the same starting point. Another aspect to explore is the back-to-front image of a reflection. A piece of paper with lettering on it will take on an abstract quality when seen in a mirror, and the words will present the illusion of being written in a foreign language. By

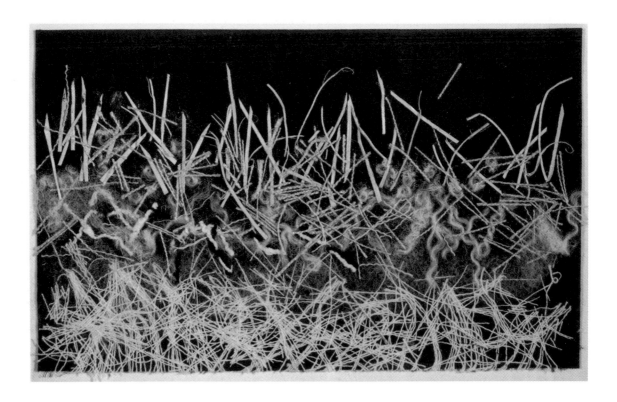

▲

141   A collage of threads and raffia is used to record the impression of grasses on a river bank in this series by Sheila Jolly.

◁ 142   Hand stitching on scrim with an applied strip of frayed fabric echoes the textures created in the collage.

△

143   Another interpretation
explores the use of frayed edges
and threads of different fabrics.
Notice the contrast of scale and
texture.

144   Hand and machine stitching ▷
on painted fabric take the ideas a
stage further. The smooth
reflections are stitched over
applied organza, contrasting with
the tangled undergrowth on the
bank.

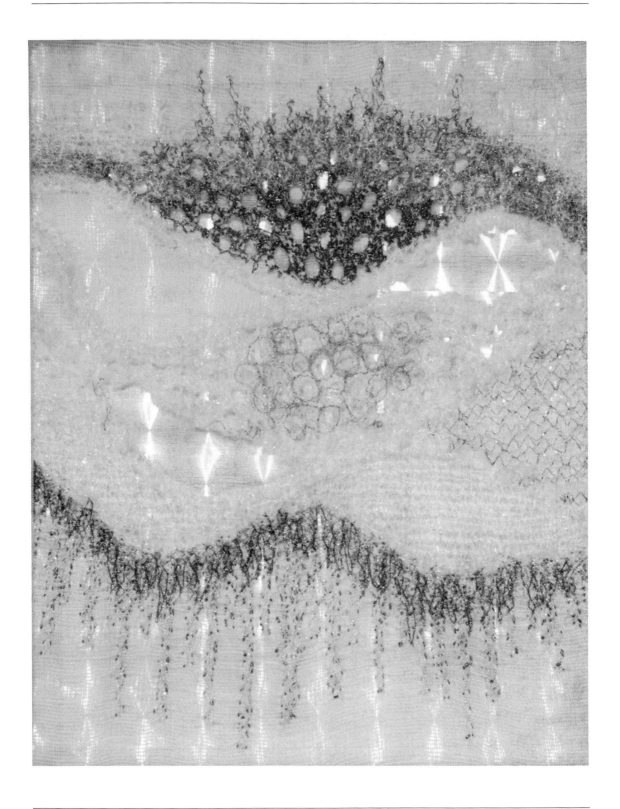

△
146   The reflections of light through a reeded glass window give a fragmented pattern of colour and tone. (*Antony Best*)

147   A line drawing of the intricate shapes seen in the reeded glass window. The distortion of the reflected light and shadow makes an interesting and unusual pattern. (*Muriel Best*)
▽

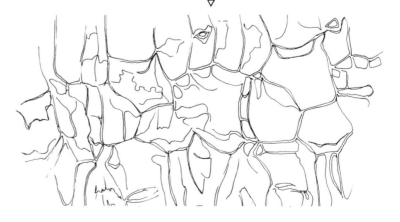

◁ 145   The reflective qualities of holographic plastic are exploited in this delicate piece of embroidery called 'Winter Reflections' by Bobby Riddle. Various machine embroidery techniques are worked on a fine scrim and laid over the plastic.

taking the actual image as well as the reflected one an interesting counter-change effect can be developed.

1. Taking the idea of the drop of water in focus against an impressionistic background, emphasize the effect by contrasting sharp images with indeterminate shapes and accentuate the changes in scale.
2. Try basing a design on the reflections that you see looking through a window, with the superimposed shapes from inside and out. Cut and layered tissue paper could help create this impression aided by a grid stencil laid over the top.
3. Using painted or printed paper make a fractured image by cutting it into strips and reassembling it. Make your cuts either vertical or horizontal and alter the image by moving them from side to side or up and down, but still keep them touching.

Interpretations

1. The technique of metal thread would be well-suited to interpret exercise 1, the fascinating miniaturized detail in the rain drop could be the focus for intricate or nué. This could then merge into a background of paint-sprayed fabric, and be highlighted with surface stitchery.
2. Recreate the effect of the superimposed shapes in exercise 2 using flat, pieced fabric within the framework of a grid. A large quilt could be made in this way.
3. The idea of the fractured image might be translated into a design for canvas work. By using straight stitches of varying lengths or smooth tent stitches, an interesting pattern of colour and shape could be achieved, creating an abstract effect of a rippling broken image.

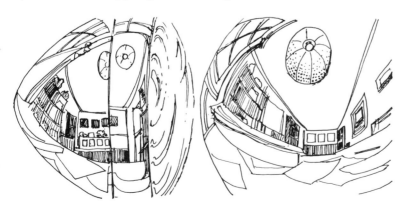

148   The rectangular interior of a room is greatly distorted when reflected in the shiny chrome surface of the head-lamps of a vintage car. (*Vicky Lugg*)

SEVEN

C·O·A·S·T·L·I·N·E·S

149   Land, sea and sky. A walk along the rocky cliffs of the Dorset coast gives a sense of space and timelessness. (*Muriel Best*)

Definition – border of land near the sea; sea-shore; the line of the shore with special regard to its configuration; strand; beach.

Ideas based on landscape are a familiar source of design, but by taking one aspect to explore, such as coastlines, many more possibilities for pattern, line and texture will become apparent. The actual structure of the coastline varies from one area to another; cliffs can be chalk, limestone, sandstone, granite and basalt. Beaches can vary from golden sands to shingle, with small pebbles to large ones, and an immense variety of shells.

In your mind's eye travel around the coastline of the British Isles, exploring from the magnificent towering cliffs and secluded sandy coves of Cornwall to the vast low shoreline of the east coast with the windswept beaches, stretching as far as the eye can seen. Look at the seaside villages and towns that provide a livelihood for so many people from fishermen to guest-house landladies. The coastline can be viewed from many angles; imagine looking along the shoreline as you walk on the cliffs, or from the deck of a ship returning from a voyage, and from an aeroplane when you can see the shore laid out below like a contour map or model. As the coastline dips and soars, so the colours, forms and textures will change. The sea itself is constantly changing from the tranquil, pellucid waters like those of a Scottish loch on a fine day, to the rolling breakers beloved by the surfboard riders, who rise like seals from the sea clad in their black wetsuits.

◁ 150   Line drawing of huts and boats by the shore. Quick sketches are always useful to keep for future reference. (*Muriel Best*)

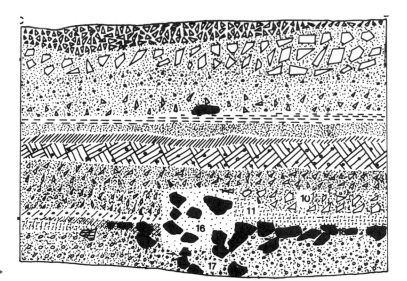

151 Stratigraphy – diagram by Philip Best of a section of an archaeological excavation, which shows the different layers and composition of the soil. ▷

152 A geological map of the Dorset coastline combined with impressions of seaside holidays was the inspiration for this small panel using needle-lace techniques. 'The Isle of Purbeck', (*Jane Swift*). ▷

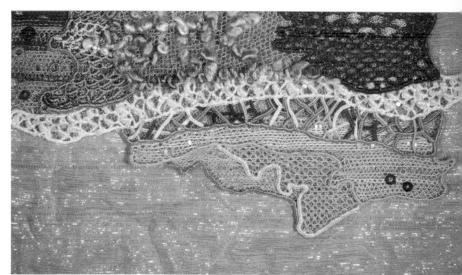

Where to look

Colour and textures make a good starting point so why not take an imaginary walk along the coast beginning on the cliff top noting down everything you might expect to see. There will be various plants, perhaps sea holly, thrift, valerian and many different grasses, with insects, snails and – on a really hot sunny day – a quick, darting lizard among the rocks and stones. The sea birds, cruising on the thermals or voraciously squabbling over the debris from the fishing boats, are all part of the experience.

Climbing down to the shore, note how the seaweed drapes itself over the rocks, its rubbery fronds contrasting with the grittiness of the sand and shingle. Notice, too, how the ripples on the sand at low tide resemble giant quilting patterns, with footprints making lines of running stitch! Smooth pebbles polished by the constant washing of the sea, driftwood bleached by the sun and weathered into sculptured shapes, crabs, mussels, shells, and barnacles all provide a rich source

153 The thrift-covered cliffs and sandy beaches of Cornwall are memories from endless sun-filled days of childhood. The applied fabrics include hand-made paper. (*Ruth Collins*)

154 Seashells can be found in countless shapes and sizes. A close study of their construction, patterning and colour is very rewarding. (*Vicky Lugg*)

of ideas.

The harbour will give further ideas, with the boats moored at the quayside, their coils of rope making interesting shapes and patterns. The odds and ends left around by fishermen, their lobster pots, nets and floats looking like giant necklaces are all examples of accidental design. The promenade of a seaside resort presents another aspect of the coastline: rows of striped deckchairs, lines of bunting, beach huts, swimmers, sunbathers, sandcastles, ornamental flower beds, candyfloss, ice-creams and splendid pier pavilions are just some of the things which come to mind. You may look nostalgically for the traditional entertainments – the Punch and Judy show surrounded by children with up-turned faces, not certain whether to laugh or cry at the antics of the malevolent Mr Punch; the patient donkeys giving rides up and down the sands; and the grandparents listening to the band playing in the ornamental bandstand.

Looking out to sea notice the small yachts taking part in the bustling activity of the regatta, their sails and ballooning spinnakers making colourful patterns against the sea and sky.

If you are able to go to the coast make notes and sketches, jotting down colours and textures; notice the patterns on the sand, study rockpools and the tiny creatures that live in them, see how the colours change from bright hues to grey/blue analagous tones, according to the season of the year. If a trip to the sea is not possible look through travel brochures and magazines for information to add to your imagination. We all have memories of seaside holidays when the sun always seemed to shine, and most families have an album of fading snapshots showing children and parents squinting in the sun and smiling for the camera. The possibilities are endless, and a whole series of designs could be built up from this one project; contrast the bright lively colours and mood of the summer with the coast in winter when the stormy seas beat against the grey rocks throwing up fountains of white spray along the deserted shore.

157 'Marram Grass', *Adrie Philips*. The combination of smooth and rough textured silk fabric and threads of varying weights creates an evocative glimpse of the sea from the sand dunes.

158 Clumps of barnacles on stones and rocks are just one of the many wonderful sources of design to be found along the seashore. (*Muriel Best*)

155 'Kimmeridge', *Doreen Harding*. Random-dyed fabric applied in flat areas over Vilene contrasts with the textured areas of manipulated fabric and surface stitchery, showing the dramatic effects found along the coastline.

◄ 156 The uneven outline and broken images of this panel by Julia Clough emphasize the empty space of the shoreline. Worked mainly in machine embroidery on painted background, the strong directional lines of the shore lead the eye far into the distance.

159 'Tobermory', *Betty Dowsett*. A wide range of stitches and applied fabrics have been used to represent the quayside of a fishing port. (*Photograph by Bill Dowsett*)

△
160   The pattern of ropes and knots are part of the scene to be found along the quayside, docks, piers and moorings. (*Catherine Turnbull*)

△
161   The intricacies of the knots used by fishermen and sailors are unusual sources of design. (*Vicky Lugg*)

162   An assortment of fishermen's huts and their boats. The weathered planks of wood, peeling paint, draped tarpaulin and general paraphernalia of those who 'mess about in boats' make fascinating subjects for observation and sketching. (*Muriel Best*)
▽

◁ 163　The seaside pier is a rich source of design ideas with wrought-iron railings, deckchairs and kiosks. (*Anne Baldwin*)

◁ 164　Deckchairs along the 'prom' are reflected in the bonnet of a parked car. (*Anne Baldwin*)

△
165　Boats are an essential part of the scene at the coast, and their shapes and colours can provide many starting points for embroidery designs. (*Muriel Best*)

166　Sturdy plants cling　▷ tenaciously to the rock face of a cliff, giving a contrast of form to the large, flatter surfaces of the rocks. (*Vicky Lugg*)

167 'Fancy a Paddle?', by Catherine Stark, epitomizes the scene at seaside resorts. Applied fabrics, striped ribbon and surface stitchery are used to create the pattern of windbreaks and deckchairs. (*Danny McClure*)

168   'At the Pier Pavilion', by Muriel Best, gives a nostalgic glimpse of the past glories of the seaside pier. Stitch and appliqué on hand-made paper, thin pieces of balsa wood wrapped with fine metal threads, and additional details added with gold paint.

169   A line of beach huts on the shore seen from the clifftop. The angles of the roofs and the variation of construction make a patchwork of different shapes. (*Muriel Best*) ▽

170 Random-dyed silks in ▷
bright colours are pieced and
hand quilted to create this lively
beach scene. The silhouettes of
the figures are applied gauzes.
(*Dee Windibanks*)

△
171 'Family Fun', *Patricia Sales*.
Simple stitchery and fabric
painting give a delightful
representation of a seaside
holiday.

△
172 'Wind Surfing', *Sonja Head*.
The shapes of applied pieces of
fabric and the direction of the
machine stitching give a feeling of
movement and vitality.

◁ 173 The bright sails of the wind
surfers create an ever-changing
pattern as they skim across the
water. (*Vicky Lugg*)

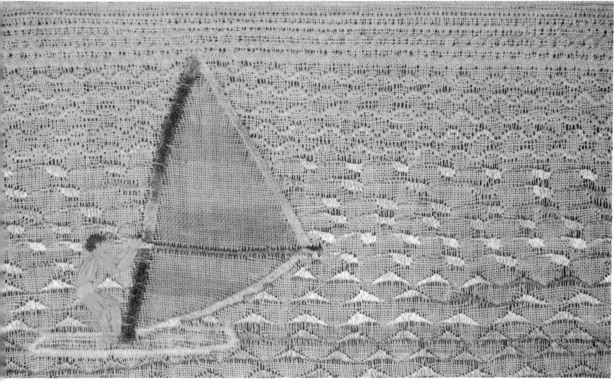

△

174　Automatic machine embroidery patterns are cleverly graded to create the receding surface of the water in this study by Doreen Bibby.

Developing a design

1. Make yourself a memory board, collect old snapshots, postcards, tickets for the pier, any ephemera that you may have kept as souvenirs of a past holiday. Assemble them on a pinboard or piece of thick card in a spontaneous, lively display.
2. Work out a set of colour schemes by wrapping card with thread. Take different aspects of the coastline, perhaps concentrating on the cliffs in summer, regatta week in the harbour and rockpools at low tide. If you are lucky enough to live near the sea, try recording the colours through the year from the same viewpoint.
3. Imagine a family on the beach in summer. See them first in close-up, filling the picture with the merest glimpse of the sea in the distance; secondly see them in the middle distance surrounded by sandcastles and buckets and spades; finally, picture them in the distance, seemingly isolated on a vast expanse of beach. Make simple drawings or diagrams that illustrate these scenes. Use your camera – a zoom lens could be an ideal way to capture these effects.

175   The shapes, colours and textures from a seaside snapshot are extended and developed onto the embroidered frame. The painted background fabric is worked mainly in french knots. (*Linda Cook*)

176   This quilted silk waistcoat ▷ by Judith Newell-Price is decorated with motifs taken from the patterns of seaweed. The colours as well as the side panels echo the pearl-like surface of the inside of abalone shells.

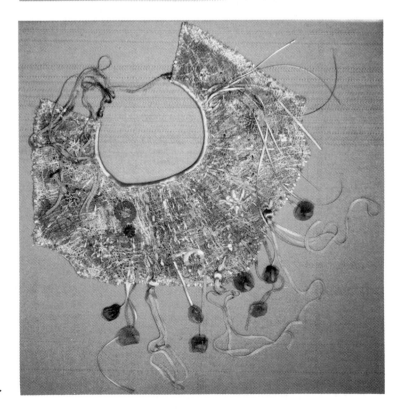

177   The collar or neckpiece is in the same colour scheme as the waistcoat. Machine embroidery decorates a loosely-woven fabric with added beads, sequins, ribbons and suffolk puffs. (*Judith Newell-Price*)   ▷

◁ 178   People-watching is always fascinating, and where better than on a beach, where everyone is relaxed and determined to enjoy themselves whether they are building sandcastles, sunbathing, or huddling behind a windbreak eating gritty, sandy sandwiches! (*Muriel Best*)

179   Drawings in pencil and pen and ink, watercolour studies and photographs are brought together to present a multiple image of the rocky Dorset coastline. (*Muriel Best*)   ▷

On the beach

Portland

Quarries

Quarry Rocks

Interpretations

1. Interpret your memory board as a panel or hanging; apply fabrics to the background, using padded shapes for some areas and hand and machine stitching to create a montage of colour and texture. Postcards and photographs could be used as they are, or interpreted in fabric and thread; fabric paint, handmade paper or felt could also be incorporated.
2. Think of the shapes, patterns and colours of all the paraphernalia which we deem necessary for a day on the beach. The stripes on the deckchairs and windbreaks, the colours of beach balls, buckets, spades, sunhats and beach towels. Take these images to make a sampler of pattern and colour using a variety of stitches.
3. Using one of your wrapped thread colour-schemes as a starting point, explore the qualities of edges found along the coastline, from the sea itself to the layered strata of the cliffs. Edges of fabric, whether frayed, torn, cut, rolled, singed or gathered could be used in layer upon layer to make an abstract hanging or to decorate a garment.

It is always worth experimenting with small samples before beginning a finished piece of work, and file away any discarded ones as they may prove useful in developing another project.

180 The empty beach at sunset has a peace and tranquillity which is in contrast to the busy activity of the day-time scene. (*Vicky Lugg*)

EIGHT

C·O·L·L·E·C·T·I·O·N·S A·N·D I·N·C·I·D·E·N·T·A·L·S

181 A jumbled collection of household articles, old cardboard boxes, even clothing, crowded between the fishermen's huts on Macao. (*Michael Lugg*)

Definition – collections are accumulations of objects; groups of things that belong together or have been brought together deliberately. On the other hand, incidentals have an element of happy accident, of the unexpected, of serendipity.

The portrayal of a pleasing group of objects has long interested artists, and is usually classified under the rather uninspiring title of 'still life'. We need not limit ourselves to the carefully arranged groups of the Dutch masters; look, as the French painter Bonnard did, at the casual arrangement of dishes on a table, even the pattern of food on a plate.

Where to look

Embroiderers must be among the greatest collectors; all manner of objects, quite apart from threads and fabrics, are carefully hoarded in the conviction that one day they will be useful. Have you ever thought that in themselves, grouped together, such hoards can make a wonderful starting point for a design with their interesting patterns and textures? Even the colours and shapes of the hanks and spools of thread that are used for embroidery can have an extra life – the inspiration for the embroidery – either spilled out onto the surface of the work table or stacked and contained in transparent boxes, bags and tubs.

The many examples of natural form that are invariably collected on a walk in the country, can be put together to create shapes and spaces with possibilities for design. Shells come in a fascinating variety of shapes with interesting spirals and stripes; pebbles are many-coloured and textured; the seedheads and pods come in an abundance of forms, colours, textures and patterns. Leaves in autumn make their own design as they fall to the ground, overlapping in some places and lying separately in others. In a more deliberate way we

182 Memorabilia from a holiday in the Far East are gathered together to create this collection of shapes, patterns, tones and colours. The fierce face ending in a bell is embroidered on the front of a child's slipper. (*Sarah Lugg*)

183   Sources of design can be ▷
found in everyday life, such as in
this collection of broken egg-
shells. (*Muriel Best*)

184   A watercolour study of
egg-shells by Vicky Lugg
accentuates the shapes of the
broken pieces and the shadows
that they create against each
other on a white cloth.

▽

185 The formal display of buttons on sale at a market stall is relieved by the variations of size, shape and colour of the merchandise. (*Michael Lugg*)

186 Black and white buttons with their assorted shapes, sizes and decoration make an interesting pattern when formally arranged. The variation of the cast shadows become part of the design. (*Muriel Best*)

△
189 'Granny's Button Box' by Muriel Best shows a delightful range of buttons that have been hoarded away for future use. The panel includes actual buttons as well as embroidered ones.

187 (*Far left*) This drawing of the black and white buttons carries a suggestion of further interpretation into fabric and thread. The raised surface of some of the buttons could be worked in padded appliqué or stuffed quilting, and others in various surface stitches. (*Vicky Lugg*)

◁ 188 A nostalgic assortment of buttons from an old button box, spilt out in a profusion of sizes, styles and shapes. From the design of the button it is possible to date the garment that it comes from, and each one has its own story to tell. (*Muriel Best*)

collect plants together to make arrangements in the house or garden.

Make a visit to a natural history museum and have a look at some of the collections from the past – for instance the cases of butterflies, insects, bird's eggs and fossils. There is the basic family connection, but the variations of colour, pattern, shape and texture are endless.

The equally fascinating selection of man-made objects is also never ending in its variety. All kinds of small articles, such as marbles, paper clips, elastic bands, nails, screws, tubes of paint, cotton reels, buttons, stamps and postcards have their own particular characteristics and qualities. Domestic items like cups and saucers, cutlery, glasses, bottles and pots are worth looking at afresh. The decorative quality of sweets and chocolates, cakes and puddings, indeed the presentation and decoration of food, which has become an art-form in itself, has a delightful potential for design.

Look around at your environment and seek inspiration from the accidental arrangements of goods stacked on supermarket shelves, the rich variety of articles sold in shops and markets, the fascinating patterns made by crates, supermarket trolleys, even traffic cones. Notice the exuberant colour and pattern of open-air market stalls, flags and bunting, flying kites, balloons, and many more exciting shapes.

190 A formal collection of butterflies in a glass case was the inspiration for this embroidery by Hilary Williams. The techniques used include various surface stitches and appliqué.

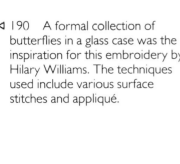

191 Fish drying on racks are one of the many examples of the inspiration for design to be found in 'collections' of food. (*Michael Lugg*) ▷

192 This detail from a collection of seedheads by Joy Dopson explores the many shapes and textures found in the garden in autumn. The seedheads set on wired stems are mostly worked in machine embroidery. ▷

◁ 193   'Fruit and Veg', *Carole Brailey*. Market stalls contain a rich array of collections and incidental arrangements, with many contrasts of shape, colour and texture.

◁ 194   'Market Stall', *Marjorie Dawson*. The panel is based on one of her paintings. A variety of materials, stitching and raised work techniques are used to portray the hustle and bustle of the street market.

195 'Three Loves, Books, Plants and Stitchery', *Mary Fortune*. The padded satin stitch of the books creates raised areas against the spray-painted background. The plant leaves are worked separately and applied. ▷

196 Hand-thrown pots of various shapes and sizes form a collection that could be the starting point for design, taking the outlines and superimposing one on another. (*Muriel Best*)

▽

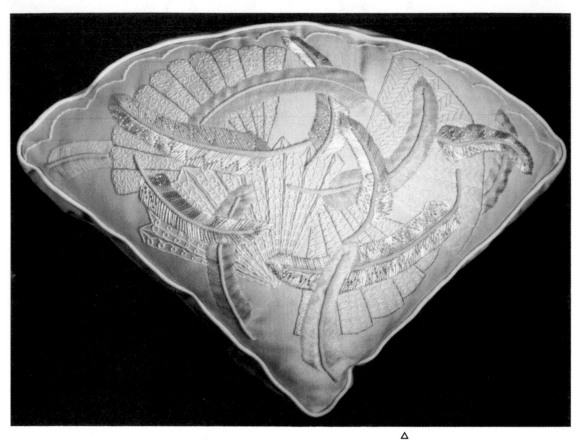

△
197   Collections of feathers and fans have been used to create a design for a fan-shaped cushion by Sue Lackie. The silk background is embroidered in a variety of soft, silky threads.

◁ 198   A design source which is close at hand for most embroiderers. Tracings are made from the original drawing and watercolour and used for a series of design exercises. (*Dee Windibanks*)

199 The dark-toned background creates an intricate silhouette from the over-lapping shapes. The hanks of thread lose their identity and become an abstract pattern. ▷

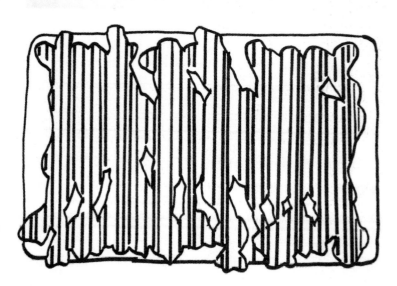

200 The bold straight lines of ▷ shading contrast dramatically with the intricate outline of the group of threads.

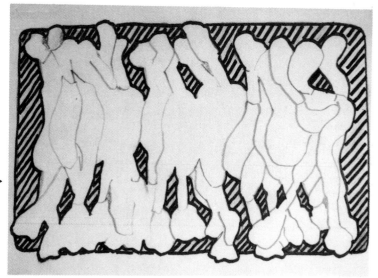

201 The patterned background ▷ dominates the overlapping shapes of the threads, giving an importance to the negative spaces.

202   These improvised washing lines bring together a delightful collection of clothing. There is an interesting variation of shapes set against a background of grids. (*Vicky Lugg*) ▷

Collections of things can be very personal 'treasures' that we accumulate through life; things that often have a special meaning and association whether it be with a person, place or event. Some things are collected because of their colour, others for the quality and texture of the material they are made from, and some because of their shape and pattern. On the other hand collections can be just an accumulation of objects and possessions heaped or stacked together without thought. A glimpse of the rows of backgardens and yards seen from the railway train, with each small rectangle filled in so many ways – some tidy, some all higgledy-piggledy – gives a tantalizing view into other peoples' lives. Sometimes there are lines of washing, which in themselves make a lovely collection of shapes, patterns and colours.

Be prepared for the unexpected as you are out and about by always having a notebook and pencil with you to jot down the ideas – do not just rely on your memory. Make quick sketches, keeping the shapes simple and noting their relation to one another, as this is an important consideration when exploring this area of design.

In your own home you can arrange and rearrange objects of your choice. Sometimes the most pleasing relations are created when the objects are just tipped out onto a table top to give an informal design. Everyone has a button box containing an assortment of buttons from garments long since discarded, and this will yield all manner of treasures, from tiny pearl buttons to large ornate ones. Try making formal arrangements too, changing the groups around, and assessing the situation as you alter the formation. You can select a small part of the group with a viewfinder or by making a frame with strips of card. It is probably most useful to make an accurate line drawing, concentrating on the character of the shapes and their relation to one another. Look for any strong characteristics such as pattern or texture, and also observe all the other elements that come into the design process. Vary the viewpoint of the group, look at it from directly above as well as from the side angles. Collections of small objects are often kept in containers and the relation of the two adds another aspect to the situation. You have only to look at the range of sweets in jars in the sweet shop, or the herbs and spices in the wholefood shop to see the possibilities in this approach.

△
203   Applied fabrics and lace form a perfect interpretation of the nostalgic atmosphere of the second-hand clothing stall with its frills and furbelows (*Carole Brailey*)

204   A sheet of drawings by Muriel Best explores the shapes and patterns created by clothes on hangers and hooks. Attention is paid to the decorative quality of the garments and materials. ▷

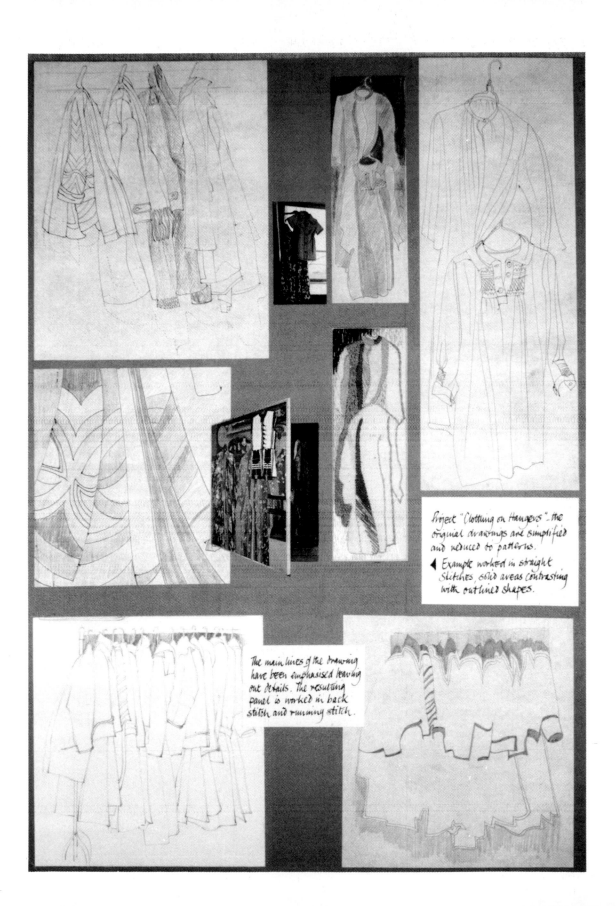

Project "Clothing on Hangers" the original drawings are simplified and reduced to patterns.

◄ Example worked in straight stitches, solid areas contrasting with outlined shapes.

The main lines of the drawing have been emphasised leaving out details. The resulting panel is worked in back stitch and running stitch.

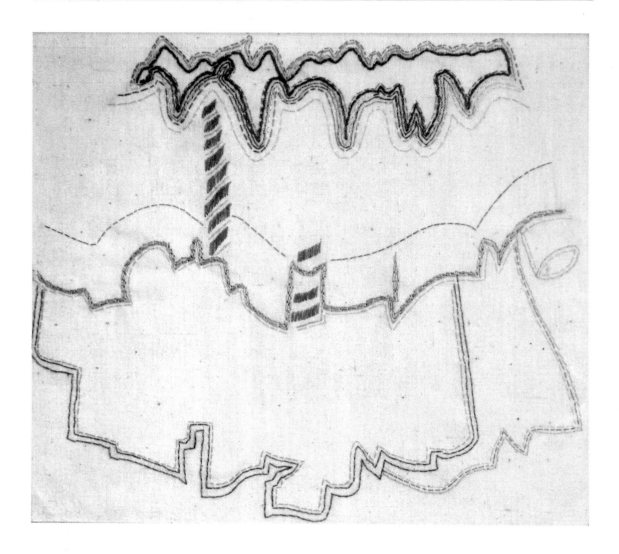

Developing a design

Assemble your drawings of both groups of objects and single objects. Choose and concentrate on one particular 'collection' at a time and really explore the possibilities contained within that group. At the same time be aware of combining images, of taking ideas from other aspects of design used within this book. For example, a design using shells could combine with a coastline project; or a still life on a window sill would fit well with the silhouette of the window frame, glazing bars and decorative blind.

△
205 The main lines from one of the drawings have been developed to accentuate the patterns and edges made by the clothing including the ends of the sleeves. (*Muriel Best*)

206 A folding, full-size screen is ▷ decorated with articles of clothing and their labels by Jennifer Hollingdale. The screen includes a mirror as well as the suggestion of shoes and an umbrella.

207 Coloured glass marbles ▷
reflecting light and complex
shadows are elevated from the
mundane objects of the
playground into precious
jewel-like beads. The directional
lines of the drawing suggest
interpretation of fine stitchery in
glowing colours. (*Sarah Lugg*)

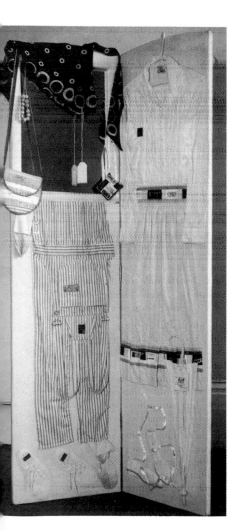

The design suggestions develop from using a single motif to more complicated, composite images. You will find that as you explore various possibilities, some objects have more potential than others, partly because of their basic shape and partly because of the intrinsic character of the object.

1. Make a tracing from a drawing of one of your objects, and use this basic outline for the following exercises:
    (a) Create both regular and irregular over-lapping shapes as required and considering the negative spaces.
    (b) Overlap the shapes to give an impression of movement.
    (c) Vary the scale of the shape to create a sense of perspective.
    (d) Use both the tracing and its reversed image to explore exercise (a).

2. Make a tracing of a group of objects and try out the above exercises with this new composite image. Also select and trace off parts of the group, using different shaped viewfinders – triangles of varying proportions, T-shaped viewers and so on.

3. Develop composite images by combining single motifs with groups of objects or repeat patterns. For example:
    (a) Combine the total image of the collection, with repeats of the single motif to form a border design.
    (b) Incorporate the total collection with selected areas for the borders.
    (c) Vary the scale and even the proportions of the various motifs and images; combine them to create further new patterns, rich in variation. Tip out your button box contents onto a table and notice the interesting variation in size and decoration.

Discoveries that were made earlier in Chapter 1, can be used to great effect in extending the potential of your ideas. Use photocopies or tracings of your designs to experiment with various combinations of colour, tone, texture and pattern. See what happens when you use a scheme of strong, vibrant colours, simple black and white, or areas of contrasting pattern. Return to the original subject matter and let ideas on colour and surfaces develop afresh. You might wish to accentuate a particular feature, such as the swirling stripes within coloured glass marbles, the surface patterns on a collection of buttons, or the delicate tracery of lines and colour on a shell picked up on the seashore.

Flat areas of tone and colour, or a series of contour lines tracing the undulating surface of the object could be used to express their characteristics.

Interpretations

The range of subject matter considered in this Chapter could not be wider in both design and interpretation potential. It has ranged from the abstract to the pictorial, so do consider the whole area of techniques, fabrics and threads which are open to you. Here are just a few suggestions:

1. The delightful 'busyness' of collections can be exploited by combining a number of techniques, such as decorative stitching, raised work with its padded and applied shapes, and in some instances perhaps the object itself. The idea could be extended even further by imitating the objects with printed motifs.

2. Try making an informal arrangement within a grid as though the objects were in a display case. Leave gaps to make the pattern more interesting; use surface stitchery, contrasting smooth and textured areas to suit the individual objects.

3. Using a shaped window, select an area from your original drawings and photographs of collections that will give you an abstract design with pleasing lines and shapes. This is an excellent method when designing for clothing and accessories; just cut out your window to the appropriate shape – a kimono is a good example.

208   The foil and cellophane wrappings of various shaped sweets create a pattern of twists and folds, suggesting the form beneath. These qualities are enhanced by the patterned background of the striped paper. (*Vicky Lugg*)

NINE

W·O·R·D·S A·N·D M·U·S·I·C

209 'All along the valley, stream that flashest white'; these words by Alfred, Lord Tennyson evoke an image of the countryside. Water rippling over rocks in a stream provides ideas for interpretation into fabric and thread. The use of stitches in different directions and tones could develop into an abstract design. (*Michael Lugg*)

Definition – Words: units of spoken language; a message; speech; verbal intention; a signal or sign; expression.
Music: an expression of sound; melody; harmony; printed representation of notes; definite pitch; composition.

210 'The Foghorn', *Ruth Pasco.* ▷
The pattern created by the sound of a foghorn recorded on an oscilloscope was the inspiration for this piece. Transparent rods are applied to a background of stitched canvas, reflecting and distorting the colours.

Writers of prose and poetry use words to express ideas and to convey messages, just as composers use sequences of notes to interpret their thoughts and emotions in music. Both can communicate mood and atmosphere, using various technical devices. For example, both words and music use rhythm and accent; a writer might also use rhyme or alliteration.

Composers use all the resources of harmony and instrumental colour; an instance being the languorous writing for the flute in Debussy's *Prélude à l'Après-Midi d'un Faune*, where the music evokes the drowsy warmth of a summer afternoon. Tone poems, pieces of descriptive music, are written in one continuous movement and interpret a poetic idea or literary theme, as in *Till Eulenspiegel* by the composer Richard Strauss. The music tells the story of a practical joker whose pranks eventually bring him to a bad end. The cheeky theme, which expresses Till's insouciant personality, tries to exert itself even in the gloom of the ending when he is about to be hanged.

In the composition *Facade* there is a marriage of music and the spoken word. The words of Edith Sitwell were chosen for their musical qualities of sound and rhythm rather than their meanings, so that they and William Walton's score form a musical entity. The repeated rhythms of the one serve to emphasize those of the other and enhance the overall effect.

Composers and writers use their media as a painter might, creating light and shade, discord and harmony, and, in turn, artists are influenced by words and music. Paul Klee is a case in point; coming from a cultured family, he was also a gifted poet and musician, and as a young man played the violin with the Berne Municipal Orchestra. His love of poetry and music is expressed in many of his paintings, for example, *Ad Parnassum* where he sought to find the pictorial equivalent of polyphonic composition, in terms of colour and form. In *Vocal Fabric of the Singer Rose Silber* the singers' initials and the vowels a, e, i, o, u are painted over a surface of delicate colour and subtle texture. The painting has undoubted similarities to the work of many textile artists now, who use mixed media with embroidery to express their ideas.

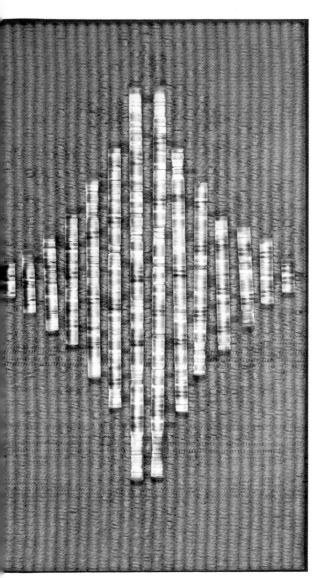

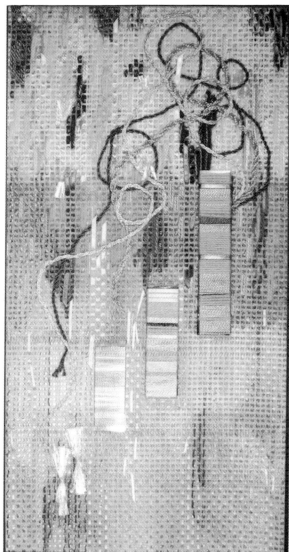

Where to look and how to listen

The images conjured up by words and music are very personal, subject to moods, likes and dislikes of the listener or reader. Everyone has a favourite author or composer; music in particular often has personal associations, and to hear a certain melody can bring back vivid memories of experiences, sometimes joyful, sometimes sad. Words will set a scene, describe atmosphere and define colours, which makes them

△
211   A lively piece of modern jazz music by Dave Brubeck is interpreted in uneven pattern darning by Mary Fortune. The solid areas of wrapped thread contrast with the fragmented stitching.

easier than music to interpret in terms of textile design. We can try writing descriptions of scenes and occasions which particularly impress us, maybe of beautiful countryside when we are on holiday, or a strikingly dramatic sunset on a winter afternoon; to read these through at a later date would recall the moment and we would relive the time again. Alternatively, we can seek our inspiration in the words of poets. In *The Shepherd's Calendar*, John Clare divides his poem into the months of the year, evoking the sights and sounds of the seasons. From 'May' come the lines:

> Each hedge is cover'd thick with green;
> And where the hedger late hath been,
> Young tender shoots begin to grow
> From out the mossy stumps below.

and from 'November':

> The landscape sleeps in mist from morn till noon;
> And, if the sun looks through, tis with a face
> Beamless and pale and round,

△
212 Words and music often inspired the painter Paul Klee. This watercolour and oil on paper, entitled *Comedy* pictures the theatrical performances which were a feature of student life at the Bauhaus. (*The Tate Gallery, London*)

213 A quotation from the ▷
poem 'The Dry Salvages' by T.S.
Eliot provides the inspiration for
this embroidery which uses
lettering as an integral part of the
design. It is worked in simple
straight stitches on a background
of handwoven silk. (*Muriel Best*)

The first extract suggests the feeling of spring when the trees
and flowers are coming into leaf and blossom; the second sets
the scene for the coming of winter with visions of damp, cold
misty days. It is easy to imagine what colours could be used to
convey the impressions: a bright yellow-green for the young
shoots, a deeper green for the mossy stump, cool greys, pale
mauves and pale lemon for the autumn. Layered transparent
fabrics might be a way of suggesting the mistiness.

The atmosphere of the city is captured in T.S. Eliot's poem
'The Love Song of J. Alfred Prufrock'. He conjures up vivid
images, writing of the evening being spread out against the sky,
and the yellow smoke sliding along the street rubbing itself
against the window panes.

A group of people listening to music might find it a very
difficult task to put their impressions down on paper, especially

214 Freely worked stitchery and barbed wire on frayed scrim illustrates this quotation 'Leave us a flower and some grass that's green', expressing concern over the destruction of our environment. (*Adrie Philips*)

215 'Rain Forest' by Joan
Matthews, developed from a
poem describing the lush
vegetation of a tropical rain forest.
Wrapped threads and fabrics,
manipulated fabric and densely-
packed eyelets create an
evocative effect.

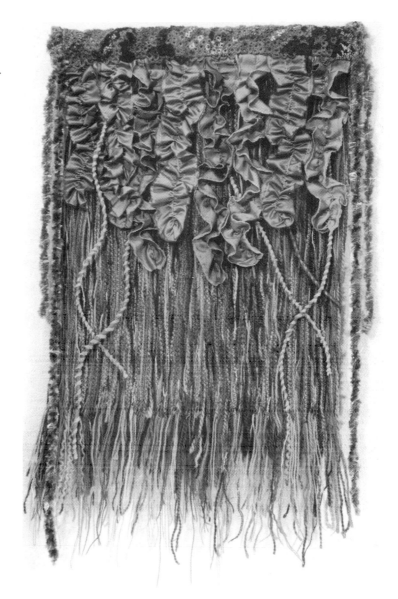

in terms of drawing or painting. Some music with strong
rhythms and dissonant chords might suggest jagged lines,
geometric shapes and strong vibrant colours, while more
melodious and harmonious music might suggest undulating
lines, rounded shapes and muted colours. The world of 'pop'
music is, in some ways, easier to translate into graphic terms.
The strong beat, the colours and flashing lights of discos
suggest a frenetic energy. Use bright primaries, discordant
colours, shiny, glittery fabrics and threads, flashing sequins
and sparkling beads, to produce a really powerful image.

216 'Charm'd magic casements, opening on the foam Of perilous seas, in faery lands forlorn . . .' from 'Ode to a Nightingale' by Keats. Strips of soft, silky fabrics and nets are applied and superimposed to create a sense of movement and changing images. The machine embroidery is worked mainly in metal threads. (*Anne Wilson*)

217 North hill north of the lake
Red balcony bright among
   the various trees
Twisting, winding the river
   to the south
Gleaming, vanishing by the
   edge of the green
   woods!
Translation of a poem by Wang Wei, Chinese poet of the eighth century AD. (*Vicky Lugg*)

218 'Titania's Chatelaine' by Elizabeth Beazley. Fine stitchery and needlelace techniques are used to decorate the seedheads that form the containers for all the items of a chatelaine, which include a tiny notebook, pencil and scissors. ▷

Developing a design

Whether you are taking prose, poetry or music as your theme make brief notes on anything connected with the subject matter, colours, texture, mood, etc. The following exercises may be useful as starting points and provide guidelines for future projects.

1. The first is based on a short poem by Edward Thomas:

> *A Tale*
> There once the walls
> Of the ruined cottage stood.
> The periwinkle crawls
> With flower in its hair into the wood.
>
> In flowerless hours
> Never will the bank fail
> With everlasting flowers
> On fragments of blue plates, to tell the tale.

△
219   The cool colours of the sea washing over the rocks are conjured up by Mendelssohn's music 'Fingal's Cave', and provide the idea for the ballet costume. The floating fabrics, metallic threads and tiny crystal beads all help to convey the mood of the music. (*Jo Quinlan*)

△
220   'A Capriccio' by Helen
Pincus, whose work is mainly
inspired by music. The title means
'according to the fancy or caprice
of the performer'. Metal mesh
and bound metal rods form the
background to the stitchery.

(a) Decide after reading through the poem what it is that
    most interests you; begin by writing down a few key
    words, noting colour and mood. Perhaps your design
    could be based on the contrast between the fresh flowers
    that fade, and the painted flowers on the plate that are a
    lasting reminder.
(b) Make some small thumbnail sketches of your first
    thoughts and then develop the one that you think works
    best.
(c) Work out your design to size using paints and/or cut
    paper – torn tissue paper is ideal for overlaying areas of
    colour and tone. Scraps of fabric and pieces of thread can
    be used, too – in fact anything that will approximate to
    your finished idea.

2. The second exercise is to choose a piece of music to interpret. It could be jazz, popular or classical; the lively rhythms of the Spanish composer de Falla, the austere tones of a Sibelius symphony or the nostalgic autumnal mood of some of Elgar's music.

(a) Write down your thoughts about the music you have chosen. Is it lively, discordant, harmonious, is the mood happy, sad, tranquil, volatile, evocative? Does it suggest strong vibrant hues, subtle analogous tones or delicate pastel shades?

(b) To determine your colour scheme try out washes of watercolour or gouache, whichever is the most suitable for the effect you want.

(c) Using felt-tipped pens or brushes and paint make marks and lines which you feel correspond to the mood and rhythms of the music. Do not be afraid of making a mess, just start again, after all it is only for your reference, and the more you work the more you will gain confidence.

(d) Combine all the elements and develop a design in the same way as in the first exercise.

△

221 Poetry can provide the starting point for a design, and on this study sheet by Muriel Best several are tried out in simple drawings, gouache, watercolour and embroidery to illustrate words by the poet Edward Thomas.

Interpretations

It is interesting to compare notes with someone who is also familiar with the music or poem you have chosen. Whether using words or music as your inspiration, avoid a literal interpretation. It is preferable to convey an abstract impression of your subject, merely taking the poem or music as a starting point. As with all designing it is a process of selecting and discarding; too many ideas and images will be confusing and lessen the impact of the final piece of work.

1. In interpreting the poem by Edward Thomas, it might be interesting to incorporate a printed motif with the stitchery, perhaps in the form of a border or frame, accentuating the difference between nature and the man-made object. Alternatively, the flowers on the plate could be in detailed stitchery to contrast with a freer interpretation of the periwinkle in its surroundings.

2. Choose the lines of a poem, perhaps the one about November by John Clare, and feature some of the words so that the lettering forms the basis of your design. Think of the letters as an integral part, with their shape and colour reinforcing the mood of the poem.

3. A simple way to interpret a piece of music is to concentrate on the rhythm and colours it suggests. Take some of the lines and marks that you made in exercise *2(c)*, and match them to stitches. Try several experiments varying the threads and scale of the stitches. Work very freely, and it may be helpful to stitch while you are actually listening to the music.

222 Marks can be very expressive of sounds, music in particular. Try drawing with pen and ink, or brush and paint concentrating on the rhythm of the marks.

F·U·R·T·H·E·R R·E·A·D·I·N·G

Baker J.S. *Japanese Art*, Thames and Hudson, London
Best M., Lugg V., Tucker D. (Eds). QED. *Needlework School*, Windward, Leicester
Comini A. *Gustav Klimt*, Thames and Hudson, London
Howard C. *Inspiration for Embroidery*, B.T. Batsford, London
Joray M. *Vasarely*, Griffon, Nevchatel
Lancaster J. *Lettering Techniques*, B.T. Batsford, London
Penguin Book of Japanese Verse, Bownas G. and Thwaite A. (transls.), Penguin, Harmondsworth
Phelps E. and Summerfield G. (Eds). *Four Seasons*, Oxford University Press, Oxford
Ruskin J. *The Elements of Drawing*, Dover
Saxton C. (Ed.). *Art School*, Macmillan, London
Shannon F. *Paper Pleasures*, Mitchell Beazley in assoc. with Il Papiro, London
Whitford F. *Bauhaus*, Thames and Hudson, London
Whyte K. *Design in Embroidery*, B.T. Batsford, London

P·L·A·C·E·S T·O V·I·S·I·T

Ashmolean Museum, Oxford
British Museum, London
Burrell Collection, Glasgow
Castle Museum, York
Crafts Council Gallery, Waterloo Place, London
Fitzwilliam Museum, Cambridge
Lady Lever Art Gallery and Museum, Port Sunlight, Merseyside
Museum of Mankind, London
National Gallery, London
Natural History Museum, London
Royal Academy, Burlington House, London
Tate Gallery, London
Victoria and Albert Museum, London.

Every town of any size has its museum and galleries and they are worth exploring as the exhibits often reflect the history of that particular area. Look at other crafts and paintings as well as embroideries, and remember to take a notebook.

S·U·P·P·L·I·E·R·S

Any good art shop will stock the design equipment mentioned in the book, and some of those listed below have a mail order service.

L. Cornelissen & Son Ltd, 105 Great Russell Street, London WC1

Cowling and Wilcox Ltd, 26-28 Broadwick Street, London W1V 1FG

Falkiner Fine Papers Ltd, 76 Southampton Row, London WC1P 4HP

T. N. Lawrence & Son Ltd, 2 Bleeding Heart Yard, Greville Street, London EC1N 8SL

Two Rivers Paper Co., Rosebank Mill, Stubbins, Ramsbottom, Bury, Lancs.

Frank Herring & Son, 27 High West Street, Dorchester, Dorset DT7 1OP

Winsor and Newton, 51 Rathbone Place, London W1

Current lists of suppliers are usually found in the magazines *Crafts* and *Embroidery*.

I·N·D·E·X